The Mind and the Way

THE MIND AND THE WAY

buddhist reflections on life

AJAHN SUMEDHO

Wisdom Publications • Boston

Wisdom Publications
199 Elm Street
Somerville, Massachusetts 02144
USA

Library of Congress Cataloging-in-Publication Data
Sumedho, Bhikkhu.
    The mind and the way : Buddhist reflections of life / by Ajahn
Sumedho.
        p.   cm.
    ISBN 0-86171-081-9 (alk. paper)
        1. Religious life—Buddhism.   2. Buddhism-Doctrines.   I. Title.
BQ4302. S86 1994
294.3'444-dc20   95-30703

ISBN 978-0-86171-081-2

14 13 12
 6   5

Cover and interior design by Tony Lulek.
Cover photo © Josh Bartok, www.shobophoto.com.

Wisdom Publications' books are printed on acid-free paper and meet the guidelines for permanence and durability of the Committee on Production Guidelines for Book Longevity of the Council on Library Resources.

Printed in the United States of America.

This book was produced with environmental mindfulness. We have elected to print this title on 30 percent PCW recycled paper. As a result, we have saved the following resources: 7 trees, 2 million BTUs of energy, 674 pounds of greenhouse gases, 3,247 gallons of water, and 197 pounds of solid waste. For more information, please visit our website, www.wisdompubs.org. This paper is also FSC certified. For more information, please visit www.fscus.org.

Mind is the forerunner of conditions.
Mind is their leader, and they are mind made. If with an impure
mind you speak or act, then sorrow comes after you
even as the wheel of the cart follows the ox's hoof.

Mind is the forerunner of conditions.
Mind is their leader, and they are mind made.
If with a pure mind you speak or act, then happiness comes
after you like your never-departing shadow.

Dhammapada, 1–2

Contents

Foreword

I f we think of religion as a belief in a deity, Buddhism is by no
means a religion. It has nothing whatsoever to do with any sort
of supernormal being.

Buddhism is a way. It is a path that leads a being to the culmination
of the mind's perfect peace, even in this very life. Rituals, rites, ceremonies, prayers, confessions, god-worship, and the like have nothing to
do with the Buddhist way of life. Buddhism has no external savior.
Instead, every individual can train to become his or her own savior. The
Buddha said, "The buddhas only show the way, you have to make effort
for yourself."

If all people follow this path, the world will become a place higher
than a heaven on earth. Though most people experience turmoil, the pil-
grim along the Buddhist path is full of peace, full of happiness, and at rest.

The way to inner peace and freedom has been expounded by the Lord
Buddha in his discourses. There are many teachers, the disciples of the
Buddha, who have trodden this holy way, and there are some who are
still treading, who can guide others. An expert and experienced teacher
is a good companion for those who follow this path.

Venerable Ajahn Sumedho, well trained under the Venerable Ajahn
Chah, has come to England and established several centers, such as
Chithurst Buddhist Monastery and Amaravati Buddhist Monastery,
with a view to teaching this practical path to full heart's peace. He has
served the country many years and has many followers. On various occasions, he has given talks about this path and its value and has spoken at
length of his experiences. This book contains some of these talks with
valuable and practical instructions.

Some writers copy theories from books and present them to the world as books of meditation instructions. But this book is not one of this sort. All that the author states is based on his experiences.

I hope this book will serve its readers in the development of their inner peace, the peace of heart that every animate being struggles to achieve.

Ven. B. Anandamaitreya
(*Aggamahapandita*)

Editor's Introduction

This book has been compiled from edited versions of talks given by Venerable Sumedho Bhikkhu (Ajahn Sumedho). The aim of the collection, which was requested by Wisdom Publications, is to present some Buddhist approaches to human situations and issues. To familiarize the reader with the basis for these approaches, we have included talks on Buddhist themes and meditation practice. This collection by no means covers the extent of the Buddha's teachings; however, it provides a good example, not only of the content of the teachings, but also of the way in which they are conveyed by someone who has been living them out for more than twenty-five years.

Ajahn Sumedho is a *bhikkhu*, or Buddhist mendicant monk, of the tradition known as Theravada (the Teaching of the Elders), which is prevalent in Sri Lanka, Burma, and Southeast Asia. American by birth, he became interested in Buddhism while serving in the Peace Corps in Borneo in 1964, and following this interest, he joined the Sangha (the community of *bhikkhus*) in Thailand in 1966. Soon after his ordination, he made a commitment to live as a disciple of Venerable Ajahn Chah, a renowned meditation master in Thailand.

Ajahn Chah was respected not only for his teaching on meditation but also for upholding the austere ideal of those *bhikkhus* who live a contemplative life in forests and remote places. He was one of a number of such *bhikkhus* who, inspired by the example of Venerable Ajahn Mun, had gone about re-establishing the strict observances of the forest dwellers. These observances included eating only one meal a day of whatever food was offered into the alms bowl, and living in a very simple unfurnished hut away from villages. Sometimes *bhikkhus* would even renounce such dwellings to wander and live under the trees of the wild forest. When a *bhikkhu* stayed in one place for a while, local villagers would discover his whereabouts and build him a platform or a simple hut, just adequate to offer some shelter from the elements. A few of these huts constructed out of bamboo and rattan, along with a meeting hall, might constitute a forest monastery. In this tradition, the resolution and willingness to endure and contemplate suffering were regarded as sterling virtues. In the words of Ajahn Chah:

> The environment was such that monks had to have a great deal of patience and endurance; they didn't bother over minor ailments...Sometimes one had to walk ten to twelve kilometers on almsround. You would leave as soon as it was light and maybe return around ten or eleven o'clock. One didn't get very much either, perhaps some glutinous rice, salt, or a few chilies. Whether you got anything to eat with the rice or not didn't matter. That's the way it was. No one dared complain of hunger or fatigue; they were just not inclined to complain but learned to take care of themselves. They practiced in the forest with patience and endurance alongside the many dangers that lurked in the surroundings. There were many wild and fierce animals living in the jungles, and there were many hardships for body and mind in the ascetic practice of the forest-dwelling monk.

In forest monasteries, there is comparatively little study of the *suttas* (the discourses of the Buddha), but there is a strong emphasis on training according to the Vinaya (the rules and observances for *bhikkhus* established by the Buddha). When the Vinaya discipline is carried out meticulously, it sets up more than an impeccable moral standard. Poverty, celibacy, and harmlessness are just the beginning of a training that defines observances covering how to wash and dry one's alms bowl, the duties toward one's teacher, the correct way to hang a robe over a line, and many more daily activities. There are literally thousands of major and minor observances. Such training is conducive to a high degree of attention and composure; it wears down the impatience and

carelessness that modern conveniences breed in us. Again, the words of
Ajahn Chah:

> Following the Vinaya means we are contained in our speech and
> action, and accordingly the mind is contained—it is collected. If
> we are skilled in disciplining speech and action, then the faculty
> of knowing—mindfulness—is sharp. The mind is as skilled as
> speech and action, and speech and action are as skilled as the
> mind. This is religious practice—training of body, speech, and
> mind.

Undertaking this training quite naturally brings you into contact with
your restlessness, irritation, and wayward impulses. Herein is the realism
of the Buddha's Way and the experiential quality of Ajahn Sumedho's
teachings. You have to know desire, restlessness, and fear. You have to
understand them fully and let go—let them pass through you—to be
free from suffering. The practice of the forest monk brings on that realization, and the forest monasteries of Ajahn Chah gave ample opportunity for seekers to apply themselves to it. Ajahn Chah advised:

> Do everything with a mind that lets go. Don't accept praise or
> gain or anything else. If you let go a little you will have a little
> peace; if you let go a lot you will have a lot of peace; if you let go
> completely you will have complete peace.

An accomplished forest bhikkhu is an inspiration to others because
he shows that such struggles do not produce rigid zealotry or cold-
heartedness. One cause for faith to arise in the Buddha's Way is the
demeanor of the *bhikkhus*, who live an austere life and yet are described
in the suttas as "smiling and cheerful, sincerely joyful, plainly delight-
ing, their faculties fresh, unexcited, unruffled, living by what others
give, dwelling with minds like the wild deer."
Ajahn Chah exemplified these characteristics. As well as living a life
exquisitely unburdened with material possessions, Ajahn Chah manifested great courtesy, profound understanding, and an enormous sense

of compassion, well-being, and good humor. As his reputation grew, people would make their way to his forest monastery. He would make himself available all day and most of the night to offer advice, admonishment, or encouragement in pithy and often humorous ways. The teachings were accessible to simple Thai village folk, dignitaries and businessmen, and even to Westerners, because the wisdom came from experiencing ordinary human suffering. The extraordinary and inspiring quality of Ajahn Chah was the resolve and clarity through which he had penetrated loneliness, doubt, fear, desire, and pain to reveal the brightness and freedom of which the Buddha spoke. Ajahn Chah said:

> The Buddha is to be found right in the most simple things in front of you, if you're willing to look. And the essence of this is finding the balance which doesn't hold and which doesn't push away.

People found the teachings and the presence of forest *bhikkhus* so inspiring that they would ask Ajahn Chah to send *bhikkhus* to live near their village, offering to provide the simple requisites for their survival. Generally, if the requests were genuine and repeated, Ajahn Chah would consent. In this way, a whole community of monasteries arose.

Venerable Sumedho stayed with Ajahn Chah for ten years, either with the master in person or in one of his other monasteries. After his eighth year of training, he was asked to establish a forest monastery strictly for Westerners, and became its first abbot. After his tenth year, he was invited to Britain by interested lay supporters to establish a forest monastery where men might train to be *bhikkhus*.

At first, this meant living in a house in the London district of Hampstead with three other Western *bhikkhus*, students of Ajahn Chah, until a more suitable location could be found. The situation was rather different from that of rural Northeast Thailand, but Ajahn Sumedho, in his own way, manifested the same qualities that made Ajahn Chah so inspiring, and made the teaching very accessible to Westerners. As word got around, Buddhist societies and meditation groups throughout Britain invited Ajahn Sumedho to give teachings. Meanwhile, the life of the

Sangha continued in its traditional way: morning and evening chanting and meditation, traditional robes, and the same observances. The *bhikkhus* went on almsround every morning, as they had in Thailand (mainly to let themselves be seen, and to maintain a continuity of observance in this strange land). It was through a chance meeting with a jogger on Hampstead Heath in 1978 that the Sangha was given a forest in West Sussex. Consequently, lay supporters purchased a dilapidated house in the hamlet of Chithurst, near the forest. In this way, the first Buddhist forest monastery in the West, Chithurst Buddhist Monastery, or Cittaviveka, was born. After years of hard work, the Sangha had converted it into a pleasant, even elegant, sanctuary for the practice of Buddhism, while the neighboring forest was made into a sanctuary for wildlife.

Since then, a great interest in Buddhism, meditation, and, surprisingly enough, the mendicant life, has stimulated growth in all directions—with unexpected results. Men and women from many Western countries, not all of them English-speaking, have come forth to request admission into the Sangha as *bhikkhus* and nuns.

The training of nuns—in a tradition which has lost contact with the *bhikkhuni* training of the Buddha's time—began to receive attention from the early days at Cittaviveka. Four Western women made the commitment to practice in the style used by nuns in Thailand. However, after a few years, it was obvious that they needed to work within a more detailed and supportive system. So a convention has come about that allows women the practical opportunities to teach and help direct monasteries, in a way that reflects Ajahn Chah's efforts to return to the pragmatic basics of the spiritual life by means of effecting change *within* a tradition.

Two small monasteries—in Northumberland and Devon—and the large Amaravati Buddhist Centre in Hertfordshire were set up to comply with requests for the Sangha's presence and teachings. Overseas, monasteries in New Zealand, Switzerland, and Italy have already been established under Ajahn Sumedho's guidance, and there are invitations to do the same in America. It sounds very growth-oriented, but the Sangha's intention is to limit expansion in order to sustain the kind of environment most conducive to contemplation. And compared to the hundred or more monasteries that Ajahn Chah allowed to be set up under his guidance, it is still a modest diffusion.

Buddhism is non-proselytizing—the teachings have to be requested— yet from its earliest promulgation, in India around 500 B.C.E., it has spread rapidly. The discourses attributed to the Buddha are still full of life and pertinence, and are well worth investigating. The advice of the forest *bhikkhu*—live simply, contemplate the way things are, and let go of suffering—is attractively clear to our confused and anxious society. Ajahn Chah advised:

> 'Speak simply, work simply—simplify everything you do so you will be able to see clearly. If you arrive at wisdom, it will be because you've learned to understand your own body and mind. To know the world means to understand the body/mind processes and vice versa…If you don't know yourself, you don't know the world…If you don't understand the nature of the world, then you do not understand yourself.

Suffering is the same, East or West, and the way out of suffering is found in the heart, not in a place, culture, or time.

The Sangha's intention in producing publications is to bring a taste of freedom to many people who live far from a teacher or who are reluctant to visit Buddhist monasteries (which are open to visitors and guests). In the spirit of the freely available truth, no charge is made for the teachings: when there are donations we produce books for free distribution. These are available at our monasteries. We have allowed this collection of talks to be distributed commercially in order to reach a wider audience, with no other motive than to help those who are interested in living more peaceful and joyous lives.

With this wide audience in mind, we have included talks that are of general, rather than scholarly, interest. Occasionally, however, Ajahn Sumedho uses Pali terms, translating and explaining them in English. Pali is the ancient language in which the first Buddhist texts were recorded.

The work in this book has all been done in the spirit of offering service. I have attempted to render Ajahn Sumedho's talks in a way that the eye can readily assimilate, while allowing the mind to hear his voice. I can only say that it is still not as good as the real thing. Several people have helped enormously in this compilation, most notably Sister Viveka, who typed it all (several times); Jacqueline Bouchereau and Chris Milton, who transcribed many of the talks and typed several of the drafts; and Joan Stigliani, Martin Kaufman, Christa Wright, and Sister Candasiri, who helped with the editing. Dorothea Bowen thoroughly reviewed the text and gave it its final shape. I would also like to thank Venerable Anandamaitreya Mahanayaka Thero, the distinguished *bhikkhu* and scholar, for consenting to contribute a foreword. May all our efforts bring us joy, and may the teachings lead us to the ultimate bliss, the peace of *nibbāna*.

Ven. Sucitto Bhikkhu
Chithurst Buddhist Monastery

PART I
Approaching the Way

Just as if a man traveling through the forest should see an ancient path traversed by men of former days; and going along it he should see an ancient city having gardens, groves, and pools; and that city came to be restored so that it became prosperous and flourishing; even so have I seen an ancient path traversed by the enlightened ones of former times.

This Noble Eightfold Path; that is, Right View, Right Thought, Right Speech, Right Action, Right Livelihood, Right Effort, Right Mindfulness, and Right Concentration. Along that ancient path I have gone, and going along it I have come to fully comprehend aging and death; I have come to fully comprehend the arising of aging and death; I have come to fully comprehend the ceasing of aging and death; I have come to fully comprehend the way going to the ceasing of aging and death.

Saṁyutta Nikāya
Nidana Vagga, 65

1

Is Buddhism a Religion?

I t is tempting to think that we understand religion because it is so ingrained in our cultural outlook. However, it's useful to contemplate and reflect on the true aim, goal, or purpose of religion. Sometimes, people regard religion as the belief in a god or gods, so religion becomes identified with the theistic attitude of a particular religious form or convention. Often, Buddhism is regarded by theistic religions as atheistic, or not even a religion at all. It's seen as a philosophy or psychology because Buddhism doesn't come from a theistic position. It's not based on a metaphysical or doctrinal position, but on an experience common to all humanity—the experience of suffering. The Buddhist premise is that by reflecting, by contemplating, and by understanding that common human experience, we can transcend all the mental delusions that create human suffering.

The word "religion" comes from the Latin word "religio," which means a bond. It suggests a binding to the divine, which engulfs one's whole being. To be truly religious means you must bind yourself to the divine, or to the ultimate reality, and engage your whole being in that bond, to the point where an ultimate realization is possible. All religions have words like "liberation" and "salvation." Words of this nature convey freedom from delusion, complete and utter freedom, and total understanding of ultimate reality. In Buddhism, we call this enlightenment.

Understanding the Nature of Suffering

The Buddhist approach is to reflect on the experience of suffering because this is what all human beings share in common. Suffering doesn't necessarily mean a great tragedy or a terrible misfortune. It just means the type of discontentment, unhappiness, and disappointment that all human beings experience at various times in their lives. Suffering is common to both men and women, to both rich and poor. Whatever our race or nationality, it is the common bond.

So in Buddhism, suffering is called a noble truth. It is not an ultimate truth. When the Buddha taught suffering as a noble truth, it was not his intention for us to bind ourselves to suffering and believe in it blindly, as if it were an ultimate truth. Instead, he taught us to use suffering as a noble truth for reflection. We contemplate: what is suffering, what is its nature, why do I suffer, what is suffering about?

An understanding of the nature of suffering is an important insight. Now, contemplate this in your own experience of life. How much of your life is spent trying to avoid or get away from things that are unpleasant or unwanted? How much energy in our society is dedicated to happiness and pleasure, trying to get away from those unpleasant and unwanted things? We can have instant happiness, instant absorption, something we call non-suffering: excitement, romance, adventure, sensual pleasures, eating, listening to music, or whatever. But all this is an attempt to get away from our own fears, discontentments, anxiety, and worry—things that haunt the unenlightened human mind. Humanity will always be haunted and frightened by life as long as it remains ignorant and doesn't put forth the effort to look at and understand the nature of suffering.

To understand suffering means that we must accept suffering rather than just try to get rid of it and deny it, or blame somebody else for it. We can notice that suffering is caused, that it is dependent upon certain conditions, the conditions of mind we've created or that have been instilled in us through our culture and family. Our experience of life and that conditioning process start the day we are born. The family, the group we live with, our education, all instill in our minds various prejudices, biases, and opinions—some good, some not so good.

Now, if we don't really look at these conditions of the mind and examine them for what they truly are, then of course they cause us to interpret our life's experience from certain biases. But if we look into the very nature of suffering, we begin to examine things like fear and desire, and then we discover that our true nature is not desire, is not fear. Our true nature is not conditioned by anything at all.

The Conditioned, the Unconditioned, and Consciousness

Religions always point to the relationship of the mortal, or the conditioned, with the unconditioned. That is, if you strip any religion down to its very basic essence, you will find that it is pointing to where the mortal—the conditioned and time-bound—ceases. In that cessation is the realization and the understanding of the unconditioned. In Buddhist terminology, it is said that "there is the unconditioned; and if there were not the unconditioned, there could not be the conditioned." The conditioned arises and ceases in the unconditioned, and therefore, we can point to the relationship between the conditioned and the unconditioned. Having been born into a human body, we have to live a lifetime under the limitations and conditions of the sensory world. Birth implies that we come forth out of the unconditioned and manifest in a separate, conditioned form. And this human form implies consciousness.

Consciousness always defines a relationship between subject and object, and in Buddhism, consciousness is regarded as a discriminative function of the mind. So contemplate this right now. You are sitting here paying attention to these words. This is the experience of consciousness. You can feel the heat in the room, you can see your surroundings, you can hear the sounds. All this implies that you have been born in a human body and for the rest of your life, as long as this body lives, it will have feelings, and consciousness will be arising. This consciousness always creates the impression of a subject and an object, so when we do not investigate, do not look into the true nature of things, we become bound to the dualistic view of "I am my body, I am my feelings, I am my consciousness."

Thus, a dualistic attitude arises from consciousness. And then, from our ability to conceive and remember and perceive with our minds, we create a personality. Sometimes we enjoy this personality. Other times we have irrational fears, wrong views, and anxieties about it.

Aspiration of the Human Mind

At present, for any society in the materialistic world, much of the human anguish and despair arises from the fact that we don't usually relate ourselves to anything higher than the planet we live on and to our human body. So the aspiration of the human mind toward an ultimate realization, toward enlightenment, is not really promoted or encouraged in modern society. In fact, it often seems to be discouraged.

Without this relationship with a higher truth, our lives become meaningless. If we cannot relate to anything beyond the experiences of a human body on a planet in a mysterious universe, all our life really amounts to is putting in time from birth to death. Then, of course, what is the purpose, what is the meaning of it? And why do we care? Why do we need a purpose? Why must there be a meaning to life? Why do we want life to be meaningful? Why do we have words, concepts, and religions? Why do we have that longing or that aspiration in our minds if all there ever is, or all there ever can be, is this experience based on the view of self? Can it be that this human body, with its conditioning process, simply lands on us fortuitously in a universal system that is beyond our control?

We live in a universe that is incomprehensible to us. We can only wonder about it. We can intuit and gaze at the universe, but we cannot put it into a little capsule. We cannot make it into something in our mind. Therefore, materialistic tendencies in our minds encourage us not to even ask such questions. Rather, these tendencies cause us to interpret all life's experiences logically or rationally, based on the values of materialism and empirical science.

The Awakening Experience

Buddhism points to the universal or common experience of all sentient beings, that of suffering. It also makes a statement about the way out of suffering. Suffering is the awakening experience. When we suffer, we begin to ask questions. We tend to look, investigate, wonder, try to find out.

In the story of Prince Siddhattha (the name of the Buddha before he was enlightened), we hear of his life as a prince in an environment where there was only pleasure, beauty, comfort, social advantages—all the best life could offer. Then, as the legend goes, at the age of twenty-nine, Siddhattha left the palace to look outside, and he became aware of the messengers of old age, sickness, and death.

Now, one might say he must have known about old age, sickness, and death before the age of twenty-nine. In our way of thinking, it is quite obvious to us from an early age that everyone gets old, gets sick, and dies. However, the prince was sheltered from these experiences, and their realization did not awaken in his mind until he had direct experience of them.

Similarly, we can live our entire lives under the assumption that everything is all right. Even the unhappiness or the disappointments that we might normally experience may not necessarily awaken us. We may wonder about them a bit, but there are so many opportunities to not look at it, to not notice. It's easy to blame our unhappiness on others, isn't it? We can blame it on the government, on our mother and father, on friends or enemies, on external forces. But the awakening of the mind to old age, sickness, and death happens when we realize that it is going to happen to us. And that realization comes not just as an abstract idea but as a real gut feeling, a real insight that this is what happens to all human beings. What is born gets old, degenerates, and dies.

The fourth messenger that the Buddha saw was a *samana*. A *samana* is a monk, or a religious seeker, someone who is devoted solely to the pursuit of ultimate reality, the truth. The *samana*, as portrayed in the legend, was a monk with a shaven head wearing a robe.

These are the four messengers in Buddhist symbolism: old age, sickness, death, and the *samana*. They signify the awakening of the human mind to a religious goal, to that aspiration of the human heart toward realizing ultimate reality, which is freedom from all delusion and suffering.

Buddhist Practice

Sometimes, modern attitudes toward Buddhist meditation tend to portray it as leaving the world and developing a very concentrated state of mind dependent upon carefully controlled conditions. So in the United States and in other countries where Buddhist meditation is becoming increasingly popular, people tend to develop strong views about its being a concentrated state of mind in which technique and control are very important.

This type of technique is all well and good, but if you begin to develop the reflective capacities of your mind, then it is not always necessary, not even advisable, to spend your time trying to refine your mind to where anything coarse or unpleasant is suppressed. It's better to open the mind to its full capacity, to full sensitivity, in order to know that in this present moment, the conditions that you are aware of—what you are feeling, seeing, hearing, smelling, tasting, touching, thinking—are impermanent.

Impermanence is a characteristic common to all phenomena, whether it is a belief in God or a memory of the past; whether it's an angry thought or a loving thought; whether it's high, low, coarse, refined, good, bad, pleasurable or painful. Whatever its quality, you are looking at it as an object. All that arises, ceases. It is impermanent. Now what this opening of the mind does, as a way of practice and reflection on life, is allow you to have some perspective on your emotions and ideas, on the nature of your own body, as well as the objects of the senses.

Getting back to consciousness itself: modern science—empirical science—considers the real world to be the material world that we see and hear and feel, as an object to our senses. So the objective world is called reality. We can see the material world, agree on what it is, hear it, smell it, taste it, touch it, or even agree on a perception or a name for it. But that perception is still an object, isn't it? Because consciousness creates the impression of a subject and an object, we believe that we are observing something that is separate from us.

The Buddha, by his teaching, took the subject-object relationship to the ultimate point. He taught that all perceptions, all conditions that go through our minds, all emotions, all feelings, all material-world objects that we see and hear, are impermanent. He said, "What arises, ceases." And this, the Buddha kept pointing out over and over again in his teachings, this is a very important insight that frees us from all kinds of delusions. What arises, ceases.

Consciousness can also be defined as our ability to know, the experience of knowing. The subject knowing the object. When we look at objects and name them, we think we know them. We think we know this person or that person because we have a name or a memory of them. We think we know all kinds of things because we remember them. Our ability to know, sometimes, is of the conditioned sort—knowing about, rather than knowing directly.

The Buddhist practice is to abide in a pure mindfulness in which there is what we call insight knowing, or direct knowledge. It is a knowledge that isn't based on perception, an idea, a position, or a doctrine, and this knowledge can only be possible through mindfulness. What we mean by mindfulness is the ability to not attach to any object, either in the material realm or mental realm. When there is no attachment, the mind is in its pure state of awareness, intelligence, and clarity. That is mindfulness. The mind is pure and receptive, sensitive to the existing conditions. It is no longer a conditioned mind that just reacts to pleasure and pain, praise and blame, happiness and suffering.

For example, if you get angry right now, you can follow the anger. You can believe it and go on and on creating that particular emotion, or you can suppress the anger and try to stop it out of fear or aversion. However, instead of doing either, you can reflect on the anger as something observable. Now, if anger were our true self, we wouldn't be able to observe it; this is what I mean by "reflection." What is it that can observe and reflect on the feeling of anger? What is it that can watch and investigate the feeling, the heat in the body, or the mental state? That which observes and investigates is what we call a reflective mind. The human mind is a reflective mind.

The Revelation of Truth Common to All Religions

We can ask questions: Who am I? Why was I born? What is life all about? What happens when I die? Is there meaning or purpose to life? But because we tend to think other people know and we don't, we often seek the answers from others, rather than opening the mind and watching through patient alertness for truth to be revealed. Through mindfulness and true awareness, revelation is possible. This revelation of truth, or ultimate reality, is what the religious experience really amounts to. When we bind ourselves to the divine, and engage our whole being in that bond, we allow this revelation of truth, which we call insight—profound and true insight—into the nature of things. Revelation is ineffable as well. Words are not quite capable of expressing it. That is why revelations can be very different. How they are stated, how they are produced through speech, can be infinitely variable.

So a Buddhist's revelations sound very Buddhist and a Christian's revelations sound very Christian, and that's fair enough. There's nothing wrong with that. But we need to recognize the limitation of the convention of language. We need to understand that language is not ultimately true or ultimately real; it is the attempt to communicate this ineffable reality to others.

It's interesting to see the number of people who now seek a religious goal. A country like England is predominantly Christian but now has many religions. There are many inter-faith meetings and attempts within this country to try and understand each others' religions. We can stay at a simple level and just know that the Muslims believe in Allah and the Christians believe in Christ and the Buddhists believe in Buddha. But what I'm interested in is getting beyond the conventions to a true understanding, to that profound understanding of truth. This is a Buddhist way of speaking.

Today we have an opportunity to work toward a common truth among all religions; we can all begin to help each other. It's no longer a time when converting people or trying to compete with each other seems to be of any use or value. Rather than attempt to convert others, religion presents the opportunity to awaken to our true nature, to true freedom, to love and compassion. It's a way of living in full sensitivity, with full receptivity, so we can take delight in and open ourselves to the mystery and wonder of the universe for the rest of our lives.

—⟋⟍—

Question: Is Buddhism primarily an inward-looking religion/philosophy?

Answer: At first it can seem like that because in Buddhist meditation you sit down and close your eyes and look inward. But actually, meditation allows you to understand the nature of things, the nature of everything.

As a human being, you're in a very sensitive form. This body is very vulnerable, and exists in a universal system that is vast and impossible to understand. It's easy to fall into the trap of seeing the world as some external thing. When you're thinking this way, in terms of inward and outward, then going inward seems less important. What you're going into seems to be small in comparison to the outward, vast universal system.

But by letting go of perceptions, the conditioned state of your mind, you begin to feel the universe in a new way. It becomes something other than its divisive appearance of subject and object. We don't quite have the words to describe that feeling except that you "realize." The best comparison I can make is to a radio receptor. Our bodies are sensitive forms, like radios or televisions. Things go through them and tend to manifest according to our particular attitudes, fears, and desires. As we free the mind from the limitations of these conditioned states, then we begin to feel that these human forms are receptors for wisdom and compassion.

Question: So what, if anything, do Buddhists believe in?

Answer: This is a common question that's not easy to answer. If we say we don't have beliefs, then people say, "So you believe in nothing." And we say, "No, that's not it. We don't believe there's nothing either." And they say, "Then you believe there's something; you believe in God?" And we answer that we don't feel it's necessary to believe in God. So they say, "Then you believe there isn't any God?" And we can go around and around like that, because believing in something is what people regard as religion: believing in doctrines and theistic positions or believing in atheistic positions. These are two extremes of the mind—believing in the eternal and believing in extinction or annihilation.

But when you're talking about Buddhism, you can't use all your conceptions about other religions because they don't apply. The Buddhist approach is from a different angle. We're not willing to believe in doctrines or teachings or things that come from others. We want to find out the truth for ourselves.

The truth of things must be available to us. Otherwise, we are just lost and helpless beings in a mysterious universe, without any way of understanding what happens to us or why things are as they are. Are we just some kind of cosmic accident, or is there something more to it? Human beings sense that there is something beyond the appearance of the sensory world. In primitive societies and in modern ones, we find religious feeling, a sense of movement toward something, or a rising up to something. We're all involved in a vast mystery, and we want to know how to relate to it.

So what can we do in the position in which we find ourselves—incarcerated in a human body for sixty, seventy, eighty, ninety years? If there is truth, certainly we must be able to open to it and know it. Otherwise, if we're just caught in illusions all the time, then it is a despairing and purposeless existence. Without truth, life doesn't mean anything, and it doesn't matter what you do; life is without any value at all. But even though you might choose to accept a nihilistic view in which life is meaningless, you still aren't certain, are you? You might prefer to believe there's no meaning, rather than believe that there is, but you still don't know. What you can know now, is that you don't know, that this is the way it is now.

There's knowing, isn't there? There's intelligence. There is an inclination toward the good and the beautiful. There is a wanting to get away from the painful and the ugly. Human beings have always aspired. We hate ourselves when we live low, indulgent, ugly lives. There's a sense of shame when we do wicked or petty things: we hope nobody knows some of the things we do. If life were totally meaningless, there wouldn't be any need for shame, would there? We could do any old thing and it wouldn't matter. But because there is the sense that some things we do are not praiseworthy or wise, we aspire to rise above the instincts of the body and mind.

We have human intelligence; we can think of the highest concepts; we can conceive in our mind that which is the best. Democracy, socialism, communism—all these come from thinking in the highest ways about what is the most fair and just form of government. This is not to say that our governments ever attain very much, but they do try. There is also our appreciation for what is aesthetically refined: beauty in music, art, and the use of language. All this indicates the human aspiration toward what is finer and better. We can aspire to a grander and more universal world-view: one planet, one kind of ecological system, one human family. All these perceptions are increasingly common now. In many ways, humanity is now a global family: what happens in Mongolia or in Argentina affects everything.

We can expand our ability to perceive, moving from the viewpoint of the individual, in which we only look out for ourselves, to that of a global view. With this view, we include all human beings in our family, rather than just our immediate family or our national family. As we expand our consciousness, we can form perceptions and concepts that are much more loving and compassionate, beyond just caring for ourselves as individuals. We can get beyond just caring for our own family, group, class, or race. We can expand our consciousness to include all human beings, and then all beings. It becomes universal.

2

The Four Noble Truths

When the Buddha had become enlightened and was still sitting under the bodhi tree, he thought to himself, "What I discovered, hardly anyone will ever understand; it's too subtle. I'm not going to bother even trying to make anyone understand; it's hopeless. I think I'll continue just sitting under the bodhi tree."

Then the Brahma God Sahampati, the symbol for universal compassion, came and said, "There are those with only a little dust in their eyes. Teach the Dhamma for the welfare of those few." So the Buddha thought, "Well, I might as well do that. No point just sitting under the bodhi tree forever. I haven't anything else to do." So he thought, "Well, who shall I teach?" After some thought, he decided that he would go to Varanasi to find his five ascetic friends, who had rejected him when they thought he had weakened in his resolve.

When he had been with these friends, he was a super-ascetic. He was like a skeleton, gaunt, with sunken eyes, because he refrained from eating in order to conquer the terrible greed for food. He was so good at ascetic practices that, as long as he did them, these five friends thought he was wonderful. However, he eventually realized what a waste of time it is to deprive the body of nourishment and make it sick and weak, so one day he ate some milk and rice. When his five friends saw him eating this, they were disgusted at his weakening resolve, so they left.

Still, the Buddha thought maybe these five people would understand. So he decided to go to Benares to find them. When the Buddha came to the Deer Park in Saranath, near Varanasi, the five ascetics realized from his appearance that he had understood something very profound and crucial, so they sat down and asked him to enlighten them. It was then that he gave his first sermon, the *Dhammacakka Sutta*, the discourse that set in motion the Wheel of Truth.

This sermon is a profound teaching, and it's a teaching to be realized. It's not a great philosophical speculation; rather, it provides the guidelines for realization. These guidelines are known as the Four Noble Truths. The teaching of the Four Noble Truths is common to all schools of Buddhism and it looks directly at the way things are.

The First Noble Truth

The First Noble Truth is the simple fact that we experience dissatisfaction, or discontent, or suffering, or sorrow. This suffering, referred to as *dukkha* in the Pali language, is something we can see directly. There's no one who hasn't recognized some kind of disappointment, dis-ease, discontentment, doubt, fear, or despair at some time in their life. The First Noble Truth means that things are always incomplete or imperfect, even when you get everything you want. Suffering doesn't necessarily mean that your mother doesn't love you and everybody hates you and you're poor and misunderstood and exploited. You can be loved by everybody, have wonderful parents, be blessed with beauty, wealth, and all the opportunities that any human being could possibly experience in life. And still you will be discontented. Still, you will have this feeling that something is incomplete, something is not yet finished, something is unsatisfactory.

No matter how much wealth, position, privilege, and opportunity you might have in your life, there is still this sense of doubt, of despair. There is still the aging process of the body; there is still the body's sickness and death. And the metaphysical questions persist: Why am I born? What happens when I die? What is death? These are the questions we can't answer: Why was I born? What happens when I die? Will I go to heaven or hell, or will I just be wiped out? Do I have a soul that goes on? Will I be reincarnated as an ant or a toad? We all want to know what happens when we die. We might be afraid to find out, but the question still haunts us.

The First Noble Truth points to the common human problem of suffering. We have the suffering of having to separate from what we love; having to be with what we don't like; wanting to get something we don't have; and just enduring natural changes of our body's getting old, getting sick, and dying. These are common human conditions that we can reflect on. So the teaching says, "There is the Noble Truth of suffering (*dukkha*)." In this, the Buddha pointed to something that can be realized by all of us right now. It's not a matter of believing in suffering, it's the direct penetration of suffering—your own misery, your own pain, fears, and worries.

Is there anyone who has never suffered in any way? This direct experience of suffering is what I mean by the way of realization. You start on this path by realizing what you can realize. You're not initially trying to realize *nibbāna*, or the Deathless; you're not taking a philosophical position, or a metaphysical position. If you were to take a position, you would tend to see everything through a bias. For example, if you believe in God, then you see God in everything, but if you don't believe in God, then you can't see God in anything. Whatever position you take, it always biases your view, and you tend to interpret your experiences through that bias. But the Buddha's way is pointing to something that can be easily recognized in our own lives, rather than giving us a position from which to view everything.

I've heard some people say that they've never suffered. It amazes me that somebody can actually say that. For me, there's always been a tremendous amount of suffering in life. It's not because of any great misfortune—I'm a very fortunate being. I've had good parents and very good opportunities for everything; I haven't been badly treated or abused. The suffering comes from just being alive. This is *dukkha*. *Dukkha* is existential anguish. It's the anguish of simply being a human being. There's a kind of anguish connected to it, even when you've got everything and life is beautiful.

Some of us have unfortunate circumstances to deal with, maybe a difficult family situation. In this case, we have an object we can point to and say, "I'm unhappy because of that person. If that person weren't here, I'd be all right." We might think that if we got rid of everything that made us unhappy, we'd be happy. But it still wouldn't be all right. Most people interested in Buddhism as a religion these days have a certain amount of privilege. They've had good educations, opportunities for wealth and travel, and so forth. But even though they've had comforts, sensual delights, and opportunities, they are still discontented.

First, *dukkha* has to be realized, made real in our mind; in other words, it has to be made a fully conscious experience. You're in this very limited condition, an earthbound body. A body is subject to pain, to pleasure, to heat, and cold; it gets old and the senses fade; it has illnesses, and then it dies. And we all know this, that death is waiting there for us all. Death is here. It's something that people don't like to consciously reflect on or recognize—but it's something that can happen at any moment.

As long as we don't know the cycles of birth and death, as long as we don't understand ourselves, as long as we are heedless and selfish, we're going to suffer. When we start suffering enough we suddenly ask, "Why am I suffering?" That's when we suddenly awaken.

The First Noble Truth is not a doctrine; it's a pointer. It's not saying everything is miserable, sorrowful, and disgusting; it's not a negating kind of teaching. It does not say that everything is suffering, but it says (in the Buddha's words) that "There is suffering." And this suffering is here within our experience. We are not trying to blame our suffering on something outside. It's not because of my wife or husband; it's not because of my mother and father; it's not because of the government or the world. We're looking at that very suffering within the mind, the suffering that we create ourselves.

The Second Noble Truth

The Second Noble Truth—that *dukkha* has an origin—is a closer look at this suffering. The Second Noble Truth is the realization that this suffering is an arising condition. This suffering is not an ultimate truth. It's a noble truth, which is different. We're not saying that everything is miserable, but that there is anguish connected with the world and with our limitations as human beings. When we examine dukkha this way, we begin to look at our limitations and the things to which we are attached, and to which we bind ourselves.

One of the things we attach ourselves to is our body. The body is something that is born, grows up, gets old, and dies, following the law of nature. It's not a personal thing, but we consider it to be so. For example, if you say you don't like the way I look, I think, "He doesn't like my face. This face is what I am. This is me and he doesn't like it. That makes me angry." If I am identified with this body as me, then when people insult it, I get hurt. But if I realize the body's not mine, it doesn't matter what people say about my face. This is the way my face is at this time, it looks this way, it's not personal. It belongs to nature, it gets old and dies, following the law of nature. When we become less identified with our body, we create fewer problems around this condition. It's as it is.

If we see our own body this way, we create fewer problems around how other people are as well. We tend to create problems with each other when we believe that this is me and that is you. If we don't agree on something, we get into a terrible fight. We become very attached to our ideas of each other and then feel disappointed when others don't conform to those ideas. How many times have we been through disillusioning relationships, expecting something from each other and then feeling totally let down? Waiting, wanting, and then feeling disappointed, because somehow there's nobody in the world who can make us completely happy and satisfied. With that way of relating, everybody's going to disappoint us in some way or another. And we're going to disappoint ourselves all the time, too, because we're never going to fully become what we would like to be, according to our ideals.

The Second Noble Truth encourages us to not focus on our ideas about things, but rather to notice their beginnings. We don't generally look at the beginning of things. We look at something, and we either like it and follow it or dislike it and reject it. But to experience a beginning as something observable, one has to be awake and mindful. We look at suffering as something that has a beginning. Then we begin to look at it in a different way.

The Second Noble Truth reflects on beginnings by looking at the three kinds of desire: *kāma taṇhā, bhava taṇhā, vibhava taṇhā,* as they are called in Pali. *Kāma taṇhā* is desire for sensual pleasure, delights of the senses; *bhava taṇhā* is the desire to become something; and *vibhava taṇhā* is the desire to get rid of something.

We can see all three kinds of desire in our everyday life. If you are bored, you seek something to eat, or you watch television, drink something, or find somebody to talk to. These are all the desire for pleasure through the senses. But after a while you become bored with sensory pleasure, so maybe you dedicate your life to becoming a famous writer, or a good cook, or an enlightened being. These are all the desire to become. When you're tired of sensory pleasures and becoming someone, you want to just annihilate yourself. Sleeping a lot is a kind of indulgence in *vibhava taṇhā,* the desire to get rid of, the desire for oblivion. But as soon as you wake up, you have to start becoming something or seeking some kind of sensory experience again, so you go eat something, smoke something, drink something, watch something, read something, think about something, until you get so worn out with it all that you go and annihilate yourself again! If you have an obsession, or fear, or anger, you have the desire to get rid of it, don't you? "I have a bad temper. I want to get rid of it." Whenever you feel anger, jealousy, fear, and so forth arising in you, you try to annihilate them. That's also *vibhava taṇhā:* the desire to get rid of some mental condition that you don't like.

These three kinds of desire are beginning conditions for suffering. The Second Noble Truth tells us that attachment to desire is the origin of *dukkha.* When we are awake and mindful and we see the beginning of suffering, there we will see our attachment to desire.

But all these three kinds of desire have a beginning. They arise, and consequently, are not permanent eternal qualities of mind; they are not ultimate reality.

The Third Noble Truth

The Third Noble Truth is the truth of cessation. When we have knowledge of cessation, we begin to endure through some of these different desires, rather than just reacting habitually to them or impulsively following them. We are less attached to the desires, less invested in satisfying them. We let them cease naturally. We endure through boredom or pain, through doubt and despair, knowing they will end. It sounds pretty gloomy if you take it too literally. But looking at it another way, understanding cessation is part of maturing emotionally.

A common idea is that everything is going to get better and better. We're going to be happier, and the more money we have and the more vacations we have, the better everything will become. We'll have constant forward progress. When we're young and naive, that's the way we think life should be; we worship youth and the arising, developing, and progressing it suggests. Yet, many people begin to get weary of it all, bored with it. It's seen as a kind of emotional childishness; and to a Buddhist, that kind of weariness signifies maturity rather than neurosis. It's a sign that you are beginning to look more closely at and gain understanding into the way things are. And when you observe cessation, when you begin to note and understand it, wisdom arises. When we fully comprehend cessation, we become very peaceful because, if we allow anything to cease naturally without annihilating it, it will take us to peacefulness and calm.

When you try to get rid of fear or anger, what happens? You just get restless or discouraged and have to go eat something or smoke or drink or do something else. But if you wait and endure restlessness, greed, hatred, doubt, despair, and sleepiness, if you observe these conditions as they cease and end, you will attain a kind of calm and mental clarity, which you never achieve if you're always going after something else.

This is the virtue of meditation. If you sit and patiently endure, you find your mind going into a state of calm. That calm occurs because there's no more trying to become something or trying to get rid of something. There's a kind of inner peace or relaxation of the mind in which you stop following the struggle to become, or to have sensory pleasure, or to get rid of some unpleasant conditions that you're experiencing. So you are at ease with those conditions. You begin to learn to be at ease with pain, with restlessness, with mental anguish, and so forth. And then you find that the mind will be very clear, very bright, very calm.

Now, the conditions that arise and pass away are not the self. These conditions include all the physical world; for example, all that we see through the eye, the eye itself, and the consciousness that arises on contact between the eye and objects. Similarly, they include the ear and sound, the nose and smell, the tongue and taste, the body and tactile sensation. The conditions also include the mind, with its thoughts and memories, perceptions, and conceptions. All of these are what we call *anattā* in Pali, meaning "not self." These conditions are not me, they are not mine, they are not my eternal self, they are not the ultimate reality. These are conditions that change. Right now, you can be fully aware of feeling, or thought, or any kind of impulses in your body—these are what are observable. And what do we observe about them? We observe that they arise and pass away and that they are not self.

Rather than saying you have to believe in the Uncreated or in Ultimate Truth or in God, the Buddha pointed to what is created, born, originated. He taught that we should look at these created conditions, because that is what we can see directly and learn from. He taught that the act of being mindful and awake to the created takes us to the Uncreated, because we experience the created arising out of the Uncreated and going back into the Uncreated.

This experience of the Uncreated, at most an ineffable experience, the Buddha called *nibbāna*, which means a calm or coolness. It can sound almost like annihilation—no soul, no self, no God. It can sound really dreary, but that's not what the Buddha meant. He was pointing to the fact that these very unsatisfactory conditions, which are ever-changing, are not self. He was not making a doctrinal statement that there is no self and that we have to believe in no self, but he was pointing to the way whereby one can see the truth. As you watch the conditions of the body and mind, you realize that they come and go; they change. There is no substance to them that you can extract and say, "This is mine." When some loud, unpleasant noises come, if you think, "I hate that noise. The world shouldn't have any noises like that. I'm going to report this to the district council," then of course you think the noise is yours. But when you recognize the fact that noises come and go and change, and if you are patient in observing this, then even the most unpleasant conditions take you to peace and calm. If you can co-exist with the material world and all that you think, feel, and experience through your senses and mind in a peaceful, calm, and mindful way, that's the Ineffable, the Uncreated, the experience of *nibbāna.*

So we meditate. Meditation is a direct looking at the way things are. We observe the pattern that is common to all conditioned phenomena: they arise and pass away (*anicca*); there is suffering (*dukkha*), which has a beginning and a cessation; and conditions are not self (*anattā*).

The Fourth Noble Truth

The Fourth Noble Truth is the Noble Eightfold Path. The first of the eight factors in the path is Right View (*sammā diṭṭhi*), which develops from having seen and experienced cessation. To have Right View requires that we be very mindful all the time. We must know that everything arises and passes away and is not self—and this must be a direct experience, an insight. Right View is based on direct insightful knowing, not just thinking and believing in the concept. As long as you don't really know but just think you know, you will always be in a state of uncertainty and be confused. This is because intellectual knowing is based on symbols alone, not on direct experience of the truth.

The second factor of the path is Right Attitude, or Right Intention (*sammā sankappa*). Once you have Right View, then your intention from that moment on is toward *nibbāna* or the uncreated—toward liberation. You still feel impulses and habitual tendencies like doubt, worry, or fear pulling you back into the sensory world, but you recognize these impulses now. You know them as they are, and you can no longer delude yourself for very long with those conditions. Before, you could get lost for weeks on end in depression and doubt and fear, or in greed of various sorts. Once you have had that insight experience and there is Right View, then there is Right Attitude. Because there is still a reluctance to put forth the effort to be enlightened, you might try to delude yourself, but you can only fool yourself for a little while.

Together, Right View and Right Attitude are referred to as wisdom (*paññā*), and they take you to the third, fourth, and fifth aspects of the path: Right Speech, Right Action, and Right Livelihood (*sammā vācā, sammā kammanta,* and *sammā ājīva*). In the Pali language, we call these three *sīla*—the moral side of the Eightfold Path. *Sīla* means doing good and refraining from doing evil with bodily action and speech. Right View and Right Attitude encourage *sīla* because once you see the truth, you are no longer inclined to use your body or speech for harming yourself or other beings. You feel responsible; you are not going to misuse your own body or someone else's, or cause harm to other beings intentionally. You may do that unintentionally, but you don't have the intention to hurt. That's the difference.

When there is *sīla,* there is emotional balance and we feel at peace. Because we don't hurt or steal or lie, there are no regrets, we are not guilt-ridden, and there is a feeling of calm, equanimity, and humility. From this feeling of peace come the sixth, seventh, and eighth aspects of the path: Right Effort, Right Mindfulness, and Right Concentration (*sammā vāyāma, sammā sati,* and *sammā samādhi*). With effort, mindfulness, and concentration, the passive and active are in balance. It's like learning to walk: you are always going off balance and falling down, but in that very process you're developing strength, just as a baby does. A baby learning to walk develops strength by depending on its mother and father, by depending on the tables and chairs, and by falling down and hurting itself and picking itself up again. Eventually it takes two steps, then it begins to walk, and finally it begins to run. It's the same with emotional balance. Once you know what it means to be in balance, then it's no problem—you can walk, you can run, you can twirl around, you can leap.

So we can divide the Eightfold Path into three sections: *sīla, samādhi,* and *paññā. Sīla* is morality, *samādhi* is concentration, *paññā* is wisdom. *Sīla* is how you conduct yourself, how you live your life, how you use your body and speech. *Samādhi* is the balance of the emotions. When you have good *samādhi,* love is free from selfish desire, free of lust and trying to get something from someone. With emotional balance there is a kind of joy and love. You're not indifferent, but you have balance. You can love because there's nothing else to do. That's the natural relationship when there's no self. But when selfishness arises, then love becomes lust, compassion becomes patronizing, joy becomes selfish greed for happiness. When there's no self, joy is natural and compassion is a spontaneous arising of the mind. *Paññā* is wisdom, knowing the truth so that there is perfect harmony between the body, the emotions, and the intellect. With wisdom, these three are all working together helping each other as one, rather than as three conflicting forces.

Direct Experience

In Theravadan Buddhist practice, these Four Noble Truths are all we contemplate. As we meditate and live more mindfully and more carefully, these truths become very clear to us through direct experience. So when the Buddha was asked what he believed in or taught he said, "I teach suffering, its origin, cessation, and path." The Brahmins would ask, "Is there a God?" "What happens to the Enlightened One when he passes away?" But all the Buddha would say was, "All that arises passes away and is not self. There is suffering, it has a beginning and an end, and there's a way out of it. That's all I teach." Brilliant minds, great intellectuals, have all kinds of ideas about ultimate reality and utopian philosophies. They have magnificent systems of reason and logic, but they don't know their own bodies and minds. They haven't learned from the conditions they experience all the time.

Those who deal with the world of ideas might ask, "Do you believe in God or don't you believe in God?" If I say, "I don't believe in God," they misunderstand and think I'm an atheist. If I say, "I believe in God," then they think I'm not really a Buddhist. The misunderstanding arises from their focusing on ideas and beliefs, instead of trying to know through direct experience. What you can know without belief is that whatever arises passes away and is not self. This is an insight you can know directly. And this is what the Buddha was pointing at.

What is it that Buddhas know that unenlightened beings don't know? They know that whatever arises passes away and is not self. That's Buddha-wisdom. It sounds simple, doesn't it? It doesn't sound like very much, but it's everything, because everything we can know, i.e., perceive, conceive, and experience through the senses, everything we identify with as ourselves, as our ego, as me and mine, has this pattern of change. It begins and ends and is not self.

What then is your self? If I'm not the body or the mind, then what am I? The Buddha left it up to you to find out what you are, because he knew how it would affect you if someone told you. If I told you, would you believe me or disbelieve me? To know directly, that knowing has to come from direct experience, through mindfulness, and through wisdom. And this is the way of the Buddhas.

Question: When you say the end of suffering, do you mean both mental and physical suffering?

Answer: The suffering that ends is the suffering you create out of ignorance. When ignorance is gone and you see with Right View, then the body still feels pleasure and pain, but you don't suffer from it. It's as it is. When you don't know this truth, then you create suffering. If the body is sick or in pain, then you're averse to it, and you feel frightened or angry or depressed about the sickness and the inconvenience of it all. That is the suffering we create. Then, because we tend to resist it, we create the conditions for more tension.

If you meditate on pain—say, if you're sitting and your legs begin to ache—and you actually concentrate on the sensation itself and accept it for what it is, then you're not suffering from it. The suffering comes when you want to get rid of it, when you wish it wasn't there, when you want to move. Then that's the suffering we produce. So consider in your own meditation: What is the conflict? What is the suffering? Is having leg pain really suffering or not? If you concentrate on the sensation, you realize that it's just what it is, but there's this averse reaction to it. And the more you don't want it, the more you suffer: "I can't stand it; I've had enough." You get angry.

I used to find a lot of anger in myself. Pain and discomfort would make me very angry. I'd be angry with people because I had pain in my body. I'd lash out at somebody, and then they'd take it personally. They would say, "Oh, he doesn't like me anymore!" And then, if they weren't being very mindful, that would upset them, and they'd go curse somebody else, passing the anger along.

In order to concentrate on the physical sensation, you have to accept it. You shouldn't concentrate on it in order to get rid of it. That doesn't work; that's still aversion. You have to accept it. In fact, you have to accept it for as long as forever. When you accept it completely, the actual sensation is still present but it's merely a sensation. You can't even say it's painful. It's just as it is. That sense of its being really horrible and painful is gone, and then the conditions that support and increase the pain—like aversion, anger, and hatred—tend to diminish.

3

The Three Refuges

J ust about every Buddhist tradition includes taking refuge in the Buddha, the Dhamma, and the Sangha. These three provide a focus for our commitment and for our reflections on the practice.

The First Refuge: Buddha

The first refuge is the Buddha, often represented as an image on a shrine. One might ask why Buddhists have Buddha images. Are they idols that we worship? Do they have some kind of divine power? Not at all; it is an image on which we can reflect.

When you contemplate a Buddha image, you notice that it's an image of a human being who's composed, who's alert and serene. He's facing the world, looking at things. He's aware of the world without being deluded or being caught in it. He's neither ecstatic nor depressed. He represents the ability of a human being to be completely calm and see things as they really are, and this provides a most skillful suggestion to the mind. When contemplating a Buddha image, you begin to feel a sense of calm. Hence, living with Buddha images is a pleasant thing; they're very peaceful objects to be with.

Of course, if we surround ourselves with sculptures showing great passions of anger and ecstasy and all that which is alluring and arousing to the passions within us, then we become passionate and aroused. We become what we look at. What's around us affects our minds. So as you meditate more and more, what you choose to surround yourself with are things that take you to peacefulness, rather than to excitement.

In a monastery, the monks and the nuns make the traditional offerings of candles, incense, and flowers each morning to the Buddha shrine. These offerings are also to be reflected on. Flowers are among the loveliest gifts you can offer anyone, because they're one of the most beautiful things the earth produces. Fresh flowers enhance whatever place they're in; they never detract or ruin anything. And in Buddhism they're a symbol of moral purity. Usually, Buddha images are of the Buddha sitting on a lotus. In Southeast Asia lotus flowers grow out of the swamps and ponds, coming out of the muck and the slime. They rise above all that and produce a beautiful flower. This is just like a moral human being. A human being who's responsible for what he does is always a beautiful being to have around. Wherever he goes he is welcomed; he beautifies, he enhances. Whereas selfish, immoral, heedless human beings clutter the world like weeds. So this is why the Buddha, symbolically, is sitting on this lotus throne: Buddha-wisdom can only come from moral purity.

Human beings can attain any level. We can live, as many people do, on the instinctual level of our bodies, following the animal instincts of eating, sleeping, and procreating. We can even go below that level to being obsessed with very low desires. Now, there are many human beings who live this way. They're not really humans; they're like ghosts living in a twilight world of obsessive hungers and insatiable desires, as addicts and alcoholics. Or they can be devils, with a malevolent energy that tries to destroy and hurt others. Just because you have a human body does not mean that you are fully human. It's not that easy. The human realm is one that is profoundly affected by morality, so being human implies something mental, also.

It's only when we decide to take responsibility for our own lives that we become human beings in a complete way. To be a human being we have to use the effort to rise up. It takes effort to be responsible; it's not something that just happens to us without effort. We have to choose it. We have to decide to be that way and put forth that kind of commitment and effort in our life. Otherwise, we'll just follow the instinctual drives, which are often on a low and indulgent level. When we put forth effort, then we rise up to a higher level. This is what the lotus or the flower stands for.

When we take refuge in the Buddha, we are taking refuge in what is wise. The word "buddha" is really a term for human wisdom; it means "the one who knows truth" or "that which knows." If you call yourself a Buddhist, you can think you've joined a religion, or you can think of yourself as one who's taking refuge in wisdom. The way to be wise is by reflecting on and contemplating things. Wisdom is something that's already here. It's not something you'll get, it's something you use. It's wrong to think you're going to become wise by meditating. Meditation is a way of learning how to use the wisdom that's already there. So in meditation, you're contemplating and reflecting on the Dhamma, or the truth of the way it is. You're actually using wisdom while you're doing that. Wisdom is not something you don't have, but it's something that maybe you don't always use, or aren't always aware of.

In the daily chanting in monasteries the Buddha is called the *arahant*, the *sammāsambuddha*. These are Pali terms for that which is truly pure and enlightened. *Sammāsambuddha* means one who's enlightened by knowing one's own true nature. *Arahant* is a word for a perfected human being, a human being who sees clearly and is not deluded by appearances and by the conditioning of the mind.

The Buddha is also called *vijjācaraṇasampanno*, which means perfect in both knowledge and conduct—not just knowing what is right and then doing something else. A lot of teachers are doing that these days. They write books and they teach and they understand on one plane, but their actions are not in accord with what they know. But a buddha is what a buddha knows; he lives that way: *vijjācaraṇasampanno*—perfect in knowledge and in conduct.

Another attribute of the Buddha is *lokavidū*, which means a seer of the world, knowing the world as it is. And where is the world that the Buddha knows? When you contemplate the question, "Where is the world?" you'll find that it's your mind. However, we don't usually think of the world in this way; rather, we conceive of it as the planet. You look at a map and you see that Switzerland is blue, and England is pink. You think of Asia and Australia and America as the world, as something you can know because you can look at a map or because you've studied history and geography. But the real world is your mind, and you know the world from knowing the mind. Through watching and reflecting on the mind, you know the world as it is, as it actually arises in your consciousness—the fears, the desires, the views and opinions, the perceptions that come and go in your mind. So that's the meaning of *lokavidū*.

The Buddha is *sārathi*, which means the charioteer, the one who's in the driver's seat. This means that when we take refuge in the Buddha, we let that which is wise be the one who leads us, rather than that which is stupid and ignorant. We turn to our Buddha-wisdom, and it trains us. By opening to wisdom, we train ourselves to live in a skillful way. We learn how to live within these bodies and within society in a way that is good and kind. We learn to be of benefit, rather than being a nuisance or a curse to the world. Buddha is the teacher (*satthā*) of the gods in the celestial realms, as well as the teacher of all human beings. This means the Buddha trains all creatures who are virtuous to see things properly, to know the truth.

The Second Refuge: Dhamma

The Buddha can be personified—you can make human images of the Buddha—but the next refuge, the Dhamma, has no personal quality to it. You can't make a human image of the Dhamma. The symbol for the Dhamma that is generally used is that of a wheel (P. *dhammacakka*). Dhamma means truth, the truth of the way it is. So Dhamma includes everything—humans, animals, devils, angels, all the gods—all the things that one can conceive of or perceive, and also, the immortal truth. Dhamma includes everything—the knowing, the truth, the conditions, all sense experience, emptiness, and all forms. Everything is Dhamma.

Meditation is a way of opening to Dhamma. You're opening up to truth. So when we chant about Dhamma, we say that it is "apparent here and now" (*sandiṭṭhiko*), "timeless" (*akāliko*), "encouraging investigation" (*ehipassiko*), "leading to liberation" (*opanayiko*), "to be experienced for oneself" (*paccattaṁ*), and "realizable by the wise" (*veditabbo viññūhi*). These are words that point to the here and now. When we're opening to truth, we're not looking for anything in particular, like focusing on one object and saying, "Is this the truth?" Opening to truth is opening the mind, rather than focusing on one thing. So when we take refuge in Buddha and Dhamma, that reminds us to be in this state of alert attention. We're not trying to concentrate on this and get rid of that; we're not getting caught in the habits of indulgence and suppression. When we do open—when we learn how to open ourselves here and now—then we begin to experience peacefulness, because we're not looking for any particular thing to attach to. We're not running about anymore; we're stopping the frantic running. So opening to Dhamma is the way to peacefulness, which we have to realize for ourselves. We have to realize the truth for ourselves; it's not a matter of waiting around for somebody else to realize the truth for us or to tell us what it is.

Buddha and Dhamma aren't just nice little concepts to chant about; they are to be reflected on. They're teachings that we examine and apply to our true experience. Rather than think of Buddha as some prophet who died 2,500 years ago, we must think of him as representing that wisdom in each one of us which places us in the present moment. We don't have to go look for Buddha in the Himalayas. Just opening to the way it is now—here at this time and in this place—is taking refuge in Buddha and Dhamma. Taking refuge is not looking for something somewhere, but opening to the way it is here and now. Taking refuge is looking at how things really are, rather than the way we might romantically conceive them to be.

The Third Refuge: Sangha

Sangha is the society, or the community of virtuous ones, those who are practicing, who are using wisdom, who are contemplating the truth. When you take refuge in Sangha, you are no longer taking refuge in your personality or your individual abilities, but in something greater than that. Sangha is communal, where our personalities are no longer terribly important. Whether you're a man or a woman, young or old, educated or uneducated, or whatever, these are no longer the important things in Sangha. The Sangha is those who practice, those who live in the right way, those who are contemplating truth and using wisdom.

When you take refuge in Sangha, it means that you are willing to give up personal qualities and demands and expectations as an individual person. You give these things up for the welfare of the Sangha, those who are practicing, moving toward the truth, realizing truth.

Paying Respect to the Three Jewels

So these are the three refuges, often called the three jewels. They're priceless jewels to which we pay respect, and by paying respect we're opening ourselves to them. The sense of devotion and respect is something very good in a human being. A person who has no respect for anything—has no love or gratitude—is a rather unpleasant person to be around. People who complain and criticize and make demands, and people who are stubborn and proud—they're people you don't want to be around. The attitude that "I'm too good, I'm not going to bow to anybody"— this arrogance is an ugly side of humanity.

The practice of devotion is to open things up, to make an offering of ourselves by bowing. It's a physical movement in which we're actually offering ourselves, this body, this human form, to the truth. We're lowering the head down to the floor, putting what we identify with at the feet of the Buddha—offering ourselves to the truth.

So this is how to see the tradition. If you want to, you can use it like this. If you think it's a lot of useless stuff, then don't bother with it. It's not something that can be forced on you; it's something you can use, or not use. It's up to you. But learning how to use these traditions takes some effort, and to use them well and mindfully gives a beautiful form to our lives. Then we can have a grace, a style, a sense of communion as Sangha. We become like one, rather than a group of individual beings doing what each one feels he or she wants to do. We learn to conform in this way, in an act of devotion, love, gratitude, and respect.

Opening to Religious Conventions

People of other religions sometimes feel uncomfortable with the Buddhist symbols. It's not necessarily a case of pride or stubbornness, but of being unfamiliar with their use. In some cases, people feel that by using Buddhist symbols, they are betraying their own, perhaps Christian, symbols. But I hope that the way I've presented the three refuges offers a means of looking at any religious tradition. With this understanding, one knows how to use the Buddhist or Christian tradition. I see the oneness, the wholeness, of it all. I don't see that Buddhism, as an outward form, is the only way. I see that truth and openness to truth is what religion is all about—or should be about. It gets very confused because people forget that, and get stuck in the tradition as if it were an end in itself. Rather than using the tradition and the ceremonies for opening themselves, they use them to hold on.

When you start attaching to Buddhism, then you're no longer open. Then you become a sectarian Buddhist. In Buddhism there are different schools, so you can become a Mahāyāna Buddhist as opposed to a Hīnayāna Buddhist, or Vajrayāna Buddhist, or Zen Buddhist. There are all kinds of variations in Buddhism. In Britain we've got everything: Christian Buddhists, Buddhist Christians, Jewish Buddhists, Buddhist Jews, modern scientific Buddhists, British Buddhists, and so on. Then there are Buddhists who aren't Buddhists because they've rejected Buddha and Sangha and just uphold the Dhamma—they're Dhammaists.

So attachment breeds these separations; it's divisive. Whatever you attach to becomes a sect or cult. The sectarian tendency is one of humanity's great problems, whether it's religious or political or whatever. When people say, "My way is right and all the rest are wrong," or "Mine is the best and the rest are inferior," that's attachment. Even if what you have might be the finest, if you're attached to the finest, you're still an ignorant, unenlightened person. So you can have the finest and best of everything and still be unenlightened.

I don't ever want to give the impression that Theravadan Buddhism is the best or the only way. Because "best" and "only" are qualities that we

attach to. Theravadan Buddhism provides a convention, something that
you open to, contemplate, and learn how to use. Whether you like it,
don't like it, resent it, are irritated by it, really love it, or are indifferent
toward it—note the condition of mind, rather than take sides for or against
it. Then you can reflect on it. It offers you something to observe in yourself. And it offers you the opportunity to direct your attention to truth.

Question: With this taking refuge in Buddha-Dhamma-Sangha, there's
a strong devotional quality, and yet from things that I've read, it seems
to me that a lot of Buddhism is very intellectual or philosophical. How
important is devotion in practice, and how do you engender it if you're
not actually worshipping or believing in anything?

Answer: I think for most of us, devotion comes from a practice of
Dhamma in which you strip away the delusions of your mind and find
more trust in Buddha-Dhamma-Sangha. You don't have to convince
yourself that there are such things as Buddha-Dhamma-Sangha to trust
in; you're not creating it out of idealism. The more you strip away delusion, the more confidence you have in what we call, in conventional language, Buddha-Dhamma-Sangha. Without that trust and confidence,
no matter how much we meditate or how much we reflect on things, if
we don't have a foundation in those refuges, then Dhamma becomes a
kind of ideal to be attained in the future, or it becomes a method of psychological releases to various situations. Either way, it doesn't transcend;
you don't realize the transcendent deathless reality. If you're still working on the level of you, as a person, trying to be free from delusion or fear
or desire, it might help you to deal with this material world in society,
but it's not a transcendent way. For that, you must have complete and
utter faith and confidence in Buddha-Dhamma-Sangha. The refuges
don't exist in their own right. They're suggestions to the mind which
help you to realize the true nature of Buddha-Dhamma-Sangha. If you
contemplate them, then all the assumptions coming from the self view
can be relinquished.

Question: Would you suggest anything, such as chanting or having shrines, that would help get that faith going, make it concrete?

Answer: Yes. I encourage you to use any art, symbols, conventions, or traditions that you find helpful. Remember, in a society where Buddha-Dhamma-Sangha means nothing and where there are a lot of views against tradition and devotion, devotion is seen as a kind of simple-minded belief. So we really need to take the symbols of our religion and develop them out of wisdom, not out of superstition. With Buddha-Dhamma-Sangha, we're not using symbols in a superstitious way, but with wisdom—for remembrance, for recollection, for mindfulness. And if you develop a devotion to Buddha-Dhamma-Sangha in the here and now, then you're using them. They become tools for mindfulness, rather than symbols for belief.

4

The Way of Loving-Kindness

M *ettā*, or loving-kindness, is a skillful means that we can use to approach things that we find annoying or unpleasant in ourselves or our surroundings. When I first came to England, I asked people, "Do you practice *mettā*?" and they said, "Oh, can't stand it!" So I asked, "Well, what do you think it is?" And they said, "Well, it's that kind of smarmy whitewashing of your mind, where you say you love absolutely everything. You're supposed to try to convince yourself that you love your enemies and that you love yourself. Can you imagine spending an hour just thinking about how you love yourself?"

I realized that they really didn't understand *mettā*. *Mettā* is not an idealistic state of mind. We can feel love for all beings as long as nothing is annoying or irritating us, but as soon as someone or something comes along and insults or harms us, it is very difficult to hold on to an ideal of loving that person or thing.

Loving Versus Liking

As it is generally translated in English, the word "loving" is more or less synonymous with "liking." We say we love things—we love food, we love drinks, we love each other; actually, what we mean is that we like things, we are attracted to them. *Mettā* is more like Christian love, although this can be very idealistic, too. Christian love tends to come from an idea of how we should feel toward each other. We are told, "Love thy neighbor as thyself" and "Love your enemies." Consider what this means. Must you like your enemies? Do you want to be near them? Clearly, "love" does not mean the same thing as "like" in all situations. In this sense, "love" is a very over-used word in the English language.

Mettā does not necessarily mean liking anything at all. It means an attitude of not dwelling on the unpleasantness or faults of any situation inside or outside oneself. Now with *mettā*, one isn't blinding oneself with an ideal. Instead, one is witnessing the unpleasantness in a situation, thing, person, or in oneself without creating anything around it. You simply stop the mind from thinking, "I hate it, I don't want it." That's what I consider to be *mettā*.

Somebody came to me just recently and said, "I have trouble feeling *mettā* for a certain person. Sometimes I just want to hit her; sometimes I just want to do her in. I can't feel *mettā* for anybody like that, and it's driving me crazy!" I said, "But you haven't hit her yet, you haven't killed her, have you?" She responded, "No." I said, "Then you are practicing *mettā*." It's as simple as that.

Mettā *and Morality*

In the Buddha-Dhamma it's very clear that morality is based on correct bodily action and speech. Now, we recognize that we can't always control what thoughts we will have in our minds. We can't say, "I am only going to have kind, loving thoughts toward everybody." We can only try not to have bad thoughts or feel anger, jealousy, and fear. But it's different with bodily action and speech. We can vow right now not to kill anyone. We can take the five precepts.

We can also vow to be careful with what we say so that, even though we are thinking the most awful thoughts, we aren't actually saying them to people. Suppose I am thinking the most awful, maniacal thoughts right now: I can just refrain from expressing them to you. That is *mettā*. The thought process and the feelings go on; I recognize them, but I refuse to act on them physically or verbally.

We begin to realize the mind is like a mirror that reflects everything. Like a mirror, the mind is not damaged by anything it is reflecting. A mirror can reflect the ugliest, nastiest thing in the whole world and still remains untarnished, even though the reflection is terrible. The mind is like that mirror; the mind itself is pure. There is nothing wrong with the mind, but the reflections can be very impure or ugly or vicious, or they can be very beautiful. If we try to punish the mirror, if we destroy or crack the mirror, we go crazy—then we are really stuck. But, if we are willing to, we can recognize that the reflection in the mirror simply is as it is. This recognition is a skillful way of dealing with thoughts and feelings that may be very unpleasant for us.

It's not difficult for me to feel kindness toward things that I like, such as kittens and puppies, cute children, and pleasant people who say nice things, sunny weather, etc. I have no problem with these. But what should I do when people and things are nasty and foul? I could dwell on the nastiness. I could think, "I can't stand that person; I hate him. Somebody like that shouldn't be allowed to live. I wish they'd go away." I could do that, couldn't I? It would be the easiest thing to do. But dwelling on such feelings of aversion does not encourage peace of mind.

Seeing Aversion in Ourselves

We always start the *mettā* practice with ourselves. We say, "*Ahaṁ sukhito homi,*" which means, "May I be at peace. May I be happy or contented. May I be at ease with myself and with whatever is going on in my mind and body." It is not difficult to be at ease with ourselves when everything is going well, but when things are not, we tend to try to annihilate the things we don't like in ourselves.

People come to me all the time, asking, "How do I get rid of anger? How do I get rid of jealousy? How do I get rid of greed and lust? How do I get rid of fear? How do I get rid of everything? I could go to a psychiatrist, maybe; he might help me to get rid of it." Or sometimes we practice meditation to get rid of all these awful things, so that we can achieve blissful states of mind and bodhisattva-like visions. We hope we will never have those nasty feelings ever again. On the one hand, there is the hope and longing to be happy. On the other hand, there is resentment and the reaction of disgust and aversion to our hellish, unpleasant mental states.

I notice that people in Britain are very self-critical, very self-disparaging. Then when I ask, "Do you practice *mettā*?" the people who disparage themselves the most, who really need to practice *mettā*, are the ones who say they can't stand it. This ability to criticize ourselves sounds like we are being terribly honest, doesn't it? We have intelligent, critical minds, so we think about ourselves in very negative ways. We criticize ourselves because a lot of the things we have done in the past come up in the present—memories, tendencies, or habits—and they don't live up to what we would like them to be. Likewise, we don't live up to what we think we should be.

Then, because we can be very self-critical and disparaging, we also tend to project our negative opinions onto others. I remember myself always being disappointed with people because they just couldn't live up to my standards, to the way I thought they should be. I'd see somebody and think, "Oh, here's one, here's the person, the truly kind, generous heart, the loving being. At last, I've found her." Then I would find out that she'd get angry, jealous, frightened, possessive, or greedy. And I'd think, "Oh, you've disappointed me. I'll have to look for someone else now. I'll have to find someone who can live up to my high standards." But then, when I'd really look at myself, I'd ask, "How well do *I* live up to these standards?" Then I could see that there were the same unpleasant conditions in me, also.

When I was trying to be a good monk, I was desperately trying to live up to an ideal. I could do that to a certain degree. Through the life we live as monks and the restrictions on it, we are restrained from involving ourselves in heavy karmic activities. However, we still have to face the repressed emotional fears and desires of the mind—we really can't get away with anything in this life. As monks, we must also be willing to allow even the most unpleasant, awful things to attain a conscious state, and we must confront these things. In meditation, we allow things that we've turned away from or rejected to take conscious form. In order to do this, we must develop *mettā*, the attitude of patience and kindness toward these repressed fears and doubts, and toward our own anger.

When I was newly ordained, I thought of myself as a very good-natured person who wasn't very angry and didn't hate people. But after ordination when I started meditating, I began to feel vast amounts of hatred for everybody, and I thought, "This meditation is making me into a demon!" I had thought, "I'll go and meditate, live out in the jungle alone, get very calm, and be able to commune with celestial beings and stay in a high state of bliss." Instead, when I first started meditating as a novice, the first two months were nothing but unmitigated aversion. I hated everyone I could think of. I even hated the people I loved, and I hated myself.

I began to see that this was a side of myself that had been repressed, expelled from my consciousness, by the ideal image of myself that I had tried to hold on to. I had never allowed real hatred, aversion, disappointment, or despair to be fully conscious; I had always reacted to it. Before I was ordained, I had a general weariness and despair with regard to social situations that arose because I had been living on the level of smiles and pleasant greetings. I had been getting along socially in a superficial way, so I had never allowed the fears and hatred to take a conscious form. In meditation, when I could no longer stop them, all these repressed feelings began to arise in consciousness.

There was resistance to them, of course, because that was the way I had always dealt with those conditions: "How do I get rid of them?" "How can I stop them?" "Oh, I shouldn't be feeling like this; it's disgusting!" "After all they've done for me, and I still hate them." These feelings made me hate myself. So instead of trying to stop them, I had to learn to accept them. And it was only through acceptance that the mind was able to go through a kind of catharsis in which all the negativity manifested—and passed away.

Being Patient with Our Aversion

The way out of suffering, as the Buddha taught, is cessation. Freedom from suffering comes through allowing that which has arisen to cease. It is as simple as that. In order to allow anything to cease, we must not interfere with it or try to get rid of it; we must allow it to go away. This means that we must be patient with it. So *mettā* is also a kind of patience, a willingness to exist with unpleasant things without thinking about how awful they are, or getting caught in the desire to get rid of them immediately and expediently.

When we have *mettā* for ourselves, we start by listening to what we really think of ourselves. Don't be frightened; be courageous and listen to the unpleasant thoughts or fears that go through your mind. Sometimes a lot of silly, foolish things come up, nothing really bad or terribly evil or disgusting, but just foolish, irrational things. Maybe we like to think of ourselves as being very serious and sincere, practical and sensible, but sometimes the thoughts and feelings in our minds are really stupid and useless. We'd like to go out and help the third world, build latrines in Ethiopia, do something useful; so sitting in meditation with rubbish coming up seems to be a waste of time. But I reckon that the ability to sit with the rubbish is a sign of an advanced student. It takes a long time for people to just let the rubbish come up like that.

Normally, you start thinking of all the important things you could be doing. "Oh, I shouldn't be just sitting here. There are so many things I have to do first, so many important things." But how much of your life is just running about doing terribly important things, trying to keep the world going, putting everything in order because you just can't face the rubbish that would come up if you weren't running around? In meditation, you deliberately set up conditions so that there is not much you can do. It's a way of giving yourself the opportunity to watch what happens when you don't have a lot of things to do and a lot of things to occupy your time. There are little things to do, like watching your breath, but you can only keep that going on for a while, until that drops away. Then you can watch the sensations in your body. Now I'm giving you another thing to do—have *mettā*. *Mettā* is being patient, being kind.

Being Kind

I have learned to be kind to things I don't like in myself. I have a character that tends to get very jealous; a great problem in my life was jealousy and indignation. When I first became a monk, I used to have this terrible problem because I hated this condition of jealousy and I'd try desperately to get rid of it. Whenever that feeling would arise in my mind, I'd just repress it. I'd practice trying to feel happiness for the person whom I was jealous of. I'd grit my teeth and say, "I am really happy for you. Very happy indeed." But I'd still feel this terrible pain in my chest and a real aversion to the state of jealousy, hoping that no one else knew. I'd stoop to great measures to try to cover it all up. I'd say "Aren't you happy for so-and-so, isn't it wonderful?" trying to get everyone to believe that there was no jealousy. Through the years, I tried to stop it, repress it, annihilate it, but I found that it was getting worse. It was getting so bad that I couldn't keep it down in any way, and it was becoming obvious to everyone. It was humiliating.

Then I reflected on it. I said, "You are obviously doing something wrong. You've tried everything to get rid of it, but it doesn't go away through all your efforts. Then I realized that the problem wasn't really with jealousy; the real problem was with the aversion to the jealousy. That was the real problem. So then, when I started feeling jealous I'd say, "Oh yes, jealousy again. Welcome!" And I'd deliberately be jealous; I'd think, "I am jealous because I am afraid that person is better than I am." I'd bring it up into full consciousness. I'd listen to it, really watch it and befriend it, rather than saying, "Oh, here it comes again; I've got to get rid of it." I'd say, "Oh, jealousy, my old pal." And I learned a lot from jealousy; it's like a warning sign, something that comes and warns you.

But to take that attitude toward jealousy, it was necessary to have *mettā* for it, a kindness, a willingness to allow it to exist and a willingness to let it cease on its own, without giving it a shove or trying to annihilate it. It was still an unpleasant state—jealousy is not a state of mind that is pleasant to experience—but it is endurable, and one can be kind to that condition. One doesn't take jabs at it and try to make it go away, but one fully investigates it. One is aware of it completely and watches till it ceases. So it goes to cessation because it is not a permanent condition of mind. It is not a personal thing; it is like a reflection that crosses in front of a mirror; you just have to be patient until the reflection goes.

—⚹—

Question: I like the idea of what you're saying about *mettā,* kindness, not grasping, and being selfless and peaceful. However, I'm always a bit anxious about just being kind and laid back and letting go. I'm afraid that everyone else is going to tread all over me. Don't you think that's a danger, that if you're just kind, everyone is going to trample you down?

Answer: Well, if you're stupid, then of course everyone is going to trample you down. If you think kindness is a sentimental niceness that you apply to every situation equally, then of course it's not going to work. Nobody can do that. And the more you try, the more foolish you are, and the more people won't have any respect for you, because it's not genuine. But real *mettā* is strong, and it's an appropriate response to life. It isn't a kind of bland niceness, but an alertness, a responsiveness to pain and pleasure and to other conditions that we must bear.

The quality of *mettā* is non-discriminative. It's because we discriminate and discern that we tend to dwell on what's wrong with everything and make problems about the injustices of ourselves or others. *Mettā* isn't pretending that everything's all right, but rather, it's about not making problems, not compounding present pain or ugliness with the aversion that comes out of ignorance. It's the ability to be patient and accept the flow of life as it happens. To carry negativity with you is one extreme, and the other is trying to pretend that everything is all right all the time. This pretense is a deluded state of mind.

Real *mettā* and real wisdom work together. When our responses to life are not coming out of ignorance, they may not necessarily be glad; they may be quite sharp and even wrathful. But they can still be filled with *mettā.* This means that they're appropriate responses, rather than reactions arising out of desire and fear. *Mettā* can be a slap, or it can be a pat. It's not in the slapping or the patting. *Mettā* is in the wisdom of the mind that's behind the action.

5

Kamma *and Rebirth*

We can speculate about *kamma* (Skt. *karma*) and rebirth, but all we can know directly is whether we believe in these concepts, whether we don't believe in them, or whether we just don't know. Rather than speculating about *kamma* and rebirth, I suggest that we study them in practical situations, investigate them in the present moment.

The Results of Birth

Sometimes, people ask me to explain why things happen the way they do. For instance, they might say, "I know this person who was good all her life. She never did anything wrong. She worked hard and was self-sacrificing. But she died in agony, of a terrible cancer. What did she do to deserve that terrible pain?" They want me to say, "Well, maybe in a previous life she did something nasty and she's paying for it in this life." That's a popular explanation of how *kamma* works, but it's only speculation. What we can say about this woman's experience is this: "It happened because she was born. If she hadn't been born, she wouldn't have gotten sick, and she wouldn't have died."

Why do we have the problems we have? Why do we have sorrow, pain, despair, grief, and anguish? We have problems because we were born. Birth conditions them all, everything, until death. If we had not been born, we wouldn't have any of these problems. This is what is meant by *kamma*, and when you recognize this, you're no longer surprised by anything that happens to you.

Somehow we have the idea that we shouldn't have to experience these things. During the 1950s in the United States, I remember we used to think that science was going to solve all our problems: in a few years we'd have conquered all mental and physical illnesses through our modern psychiatry and drugs. There would be no old age. When you had a defective liver, science was going to discover a new material to replace it; science would come up with a quick solution so you wouldn't have to die. And there would be material prosperity; everybody would have money, cars, and beautiful homes. Technology would have created a wonderful paradise.

But forty years later, what do we have? There's an increase in mental illness. Sickness is just as much a problem as ever. There's still old age. And death, the inevitable end of the body, is as much a presence as it ever was. So, in spite of all our efforts, the result of being born is that the body dies. Birth—as a human being with a body and mind—conditions old age, sickness, and death. This is one way to explain the meaning of *kamma*: what happens to us is the result of birth.

The Results of Action

Another explanation of *kamma* is: "If you do good actions, you get a good result. If you do bad actions, you get a bad result." But people are not sure how to interpret this. They might say, "Well I know someone who is really bad—he cheats and lies and steals—and yet he is very rich. He lives in a beautiful house, has every material thing he could want, and yet he's a gangster. Now if the law of *kamma* were true—good actions bring good results, and bad actions bring bad results—why isn't he suffering? Why does he have all these wonderful things and doesn't seem to get caught?" It seems as if he's getting good results from bad actions, doesn't it? You might think that because he has a big car, a beautiful house, and a lot of money, that somehow he's a happy person. But if you'd been a thief or a killer, you would realize that the resultant *kamma* is that you've got the memories of what you've done. Even if you have a lovely house and wonderful things, you have the memories of how you acquired all this—how many people you've taken advantage of, lied to, and so forth. Do you think you're going to feel very happy or safe while you're sitting in your elegant living room? Think about what criminals have to do: they have to drink all the time, take sedatives, have burglar alarms, live with big dogs that bark, and bodyguards. Wherever they are, they have to go incognito and sneak around.

Reflect on your own experience. If you tell lies or gossip about someone, or take some little thing—when you sit and meditate, does it make you feel good? Or is it something you don't even want to know about, that you'd like to forget? We should keep in mind the fact that we'll have to remember whatever we do. If we do bad things, then we have bad memories; if we do good things, we have good memories. It's as simple as that.

If you do good things, if you're kind and generous, and you sit in meditation, the memory arises, "I just helped someone; I did something good." What comes is a happy feeling. That happy feeling helps in meditation. There is a kind of joy, a rapture, that comes from reflecting on the good deeds you've done; it is one of the factors of enlightenment. This is the kind of *kamma* that you can prove to yourself, not through believing what I say, but by observing and reflecting on how it works in your own life.

So whatever you are conscious of right now, that is *kamma*. You can witness right now the results of your life so far: your confusion, happiness, doubts, worries, fears, and desires. These come from having been born, from having performed particular actions, and also from having been conditioned by our society to believe, accept, or fear according to its values.

Nationality, the fashions of the time, education, all of these have a tremendous effect on the mind. And the delusions of our times can overwhelm us. We tend to make all kinds of sacrifices and compromises in order to be accepted and to fit in. Our minds are very much conditioned by our environment and, because we're so involved with the conditions that have been put into our minds, we don't really know our minds anymore. We have forgotten the ultimate reality that is beyond the conditions; we've lost touch with the Unconditioned.

If you live more carefully, more responsibly, more kindly, you're going to feel happiness—that's the karmic result. Maybe there will still be unfortunate things happening: it doesn't mean you're going to get away from pain and sickness and so forth. But you needn't create sorrow, despair, and anguish in your mind. If you live wisely, you can refrain from getting caught up in conditions that bring these unhappy states. Your body, having been born, inevitably has to reap karmic results, such as old age, sickness, and death. But as you understand this, and you no longer seek your identity in the body, then you don't expect it to be otherwise. You're at peace with the changing nature and karmic condition of the human body. You aren't demanding that it be otherwise. You can cope with it.

Reincarnation Versus Rebirth

With regard to reincarnation, people often ask, "If there isn't any soul, how can anything be reborn? What carries through from one life to the next if there is no soul?" Now the teaching of reincarnation is not really a Buddhist teaching at all—it's Hindu. In the Hindu treatment of reincarnation, you go from one body to another. If you're born into a low caste, you must wait for the next reincarnation, your next lifetime, when you might be reborn into a higher caste.

In Buddhism, that would be considered superstition because it cannot be proved, and it tends to make one think that there is a purity in being born in a certain class or caste. We can all see that people born into the brahmin caste can be just as nasty, rotten, and impure as the meanest untouchable person. And we know that untouchable people can be pure of heart, if they live good lives and use wisdom.

Actually, the term "brahmin" means "pure," "the purified one." The Buddha said that it refers to the pure of heart. It's a mental quality, not a matter of class or caste. It's not physical, and classes and castes are not pure in themselves. They're just perceptions to which we ascribe certain qualities, and how we do that is entirely dependent on our belief. So purity is a mental quality. Buddhists don't use the term "reincarnation" at all. We use the word "rebirth," and rebirth is mental, not physical. So compassion, kindness, generosity, and morality are the way toward being reborn in a pure condition.

Rebirth Right Now

You can see rebirth directly; you don't have to believe in a theory of rebirth. Rebirth is something that occurs in what you are doing all the time. Now, since there is no self, there is nothing to be reborn as a personal essence or soul, carrying through from one lifetime to the next. However, desire is being reborn; it is constantly looking for something to absorb into or something to become.

If you are unhappy and depressed, you look for something that you can absorb into that will give you some happy feeling, or at least get you away from the unpleasantness of the moment. That's rebirth. When you are frightened or uncertain, you have to try to do something to get away from it, to make yourself sure and safe. When you are bored, you have to do something to get out of that.

Just notice in your own life how you have become accustomed to certain habits. For example, when you go home at night, you go to the refrigerator and get something to eat. You're reborn as you absorb into the pleasures of eating. Now when you've had enough of this birth—you've had three ham sandwiches, four McDonald's hamburgers, and two pizzas—you can't stand to be reborn into another pizza. Then you seek a new birth in the television set, because when you are bored, you want to find some other place to be reborn again. So you get reborn into the things that are going on in the television set. When the romantic scenes are going on in the film, you feel that you are absorbed into the romance itself. You're feeling the joy of that kiss. When he deserts her for someone else, you're feeling the pain and sorrow, the anger and resentment. Then you get satiated, weary of television, and you read a book. But you can only be interested in that for a while before you become bored again, so you turn on your stereo, which has speakers all around the room, and you blast yourself for a while. And then you have a drink with a cigarette, and you call your friend on the telephone. You look into the mirror for a while, but soon you are bored again. You can't stand the idea of being born again, and you say to yourself, "I just want not to exist." You don't actually think this—it's just a habit. So you go up to your room and crash out on your bed and annihilate yourself with sleep.

We have lots of modern toys in our society. We can buy them, own them, and absorb into them, just by turning a switch. When we get bored, we can very quickly absorb into something more interesting. But even with this quick gratification, we tend to get bored again quickly. The more instantaneous life becomes, the more boring it becomes. How much TV, food, drugs, sex, and so on can one have without becoming weary and bored with them? How much can you take before you want not to exist anymore, before you want to be annihilated? And so you have to go to sleep or take drugs that knock you out. This is what we can witness as rebirth. Rebirth is trying to become something right now. You are not content, not at peace with the way things are. You want things to be different; you want to become something else.

Sleep for most people is annihilation. You don't have to be anything when you are asleep. You don't have to put forth any effort. Being reborn all the time gets boring, so you want to not exist anymore. So there is the desire not to be, the desire to be annihilated and destroyed. You can take all kinds of drugs now that knock you out for hours on end. But you can't sleep all the time. The result of falling asleep is that you have to wake up again, which means that you are back trying to become again. So you follow the momentum of habit, trying to find something to do.

Rebirth Based on Desire

Thus, we experience three kinds of desire: *kāma taṇhā*, the desire for sense pleasures or sensory experience; *bhava taṇhā*, the desire for becoming; and *vibhava taṇhā*, the desire for annihilation. These three kinds of desire are the causes of rebirth. In fact, it's desire that's being reborn. In heedless beings—those who are not awake, who do not understand truth, and who are not mindful—the rebirth process carries on and on and on and on. It continues in the sense worlds, the realms of sensory or intellectual pleasures.

We can watch this rebirth process in our own minds. What is it that goes from the refrigerator to the television set? Is that a person? Is that what your soul is, your true essence that is going to be carried on through eternity? Or is it desire? Isn't it just an aimless wandering, a habitual search for something to do, something to absorb into?

You can watch desire in your own mind. When you are frightened, you can see yourself looking for something certain. When you don't know what to do, you can feel the momentum of desire looking for any old thing of interest. You start picking up things, twiddling your thumbs—just to be doing something. This constant activity is just the force of habit, isn't it? You don't really know what you're doing most of the time; you just do these things out of habit.

We like to absorb into things that have glamour and excitement. So we go to war films to be excited. When we see a newspaper headline about atrocity, rape, or murder, we think we've got to read that. Violence and sex, all these things are exciting. Excitement is very compelling; it has a frantic vibration. It's easy to absorb into something exciting because excitement has its own kind of energy. You can be energized through the exciting conditions around you. Yet, when you look at excitement, you see that it keeps you in a state of constant movement. Too much adventure, romance, and excitement just wears you out because you get so caught in it. You're pulled along by it, and you have no way to resist or let go of it. If you have no wisdom, you just get pulled along into one rebirth after another. These rebirths—based on desire—are the ones you can witness through meditation. When you see them, you understand what rebirth is.

If you understand rebirth on the everyday level, you'll appreciate how it must operate at the time of death. The last wish of a person, if they're heedless and full of desire, is probably to be reborn again, to find another human birth, to find some womb to jump into. This is desire; it operates as an energy in the universe.

The desire for rebirth at the time of death is a desire to be reborn again in the human form. We can only know this through watching how our own minds work. If you were dying and you didn't want to die, what would be the most likely thing to arise in your mind? It would be a desire to cling to some form of life. Some passion of your life would arise in your dying moment, and that desire would be for some form of materialization. The momentum of your habits are always materializing in forms, aren't they? You're always seeking what you desire, either a sense desire, or an intellectual desire, or a desire to repress something you don't like.

But if you are mindful when you die, if there's no longing to have another birth or to take some action, what is there to be reborn again? If you're at peace with the dying process of your body, what can be reborn? Because there is no desire, there is only mindfulness and wisdom. Then there is release, surrender, and liberation from the heaviness of the human body.

Past and Future Lives

I am not treating *kamma* and rebirth as exotic religious subjects; I'm bringing them down to a practical level, so that we can see how they operate. As human beings, we have to learn from our life right now.

It's no good to speculate about who you'll be in your next life. I think that's a waste of time, and the Buddha said it was futile to try to figure out what you were in a previous life. I'm sometimes asked if I've had any past-life experiences. I haven't. I don't know anything about previous lives, but I could speculate about them. Even if I remembered that in a previous lifetime I had been Napoleon, what would I remember? I'd just have ordinary memories of that time, being an emperor, being responsible for a lot of misery.

Now in this lifetime, I've lived a good many years and I have memories of this lifetime. Fifty years ago, I was a boy studying in a grammar school in Seattle, Washington in the United States. My name was Robert. When I was eight years old, I went to a school called John Mill Grade School, and I had a teacher called Miss Depenbrock. That might not impress anyone compared to, say, my remembering the war with Russia in 1812. But that's what I can remember—being eight-year-old Robert Jackman in a school in Seattle.

You might say, "What does eight-year-old Robert have to do with Napoleon?" What both have in common is that they are memories. If I could actually remember being Napoleon, and then I could remember being Robert Jackman, they would simply be two memories. Both memories would arise here and now. And that's all you have to know. It doesn't matter whether your name was Napoleon or Robert Jackman, Sidney or Rachel, or the Queen of Sheba. It's true that being Napoleon is somehow more impressive to most people than being Robert—unless Robert is the name of the latest rock star. But all you need to know is that memory is memory. Memories come up from thirty years ago, twenty years ago, ten years ago, and yesterday. They're all memories that come up now about previous lives. The memories arise and pass away, and they are not self.

People also wonder, "What will happen to me in the future when I die? You might say, "I've done a terrible thing in my life. What will happen to me in the next life? Will I go to hell? Will I be reborn as a toad?" You can speculate about it, but the result of having done something bad in the past is fear in the present—you're frightened right now. The future will always be unknown, uncertain, and mysterious. You could project anything from your past into the future; in fact, we do this all the time. We fill the emptiness of the future with all kinds of ideas, fears, and fantasies—but it's always in the present that we project this way.

In meditation, we can see memories of the past simply as memories, and we can see our fears for the future simply as projections. It's in the present moment that we must act with mindfulness and wisdom. Meditation gives us the truth beyond doubt and makes us responsible for how we live—not because we're afraid that somebody is going to spank us if we don't behave morally, but because it's the right thing to do. Through understanding the law of *kamma* and rebirth we know better how to live, and we skillfully use the conditions of our bodies and minds. This is the perfection of the human *kamma*. The perfection of the human *kamma* is enlightenment, which is really nothing more than growing up and being a mature human being.

Question: If there's no self or soul in the Buddhist way of seeing things, who or what is getting reborn? Who or what gets the results of good or bad deeds?

Answer: Well you see, in the ultimate sense, there's nobody to get reborn and nobody to get the results. What gets reborn are desires repeating themselves. Out of ignorance, these desires are created, and they give the impression of somebody who has problems, somebody who is unhappy or depressed. Because of these desires, it seems as if life should be something other than what it is. The rebirth process is not anybody's; it's just a process of causal conditions.

With mindfulness, you realize that the results of birth and past actions happen this way. And if you keep mindful of that fact, you don't create anybody to get born again. You don't create the illusion of anyone who's receiving anything, becoming anything, or being punished for anything. It's merely that the present moment is the result of past action. If we are not ignorant, we don't suffer from the present conditions that we're experiencing. This is very hard to understand from the personal view, so popular Buddhism teaches simply: if you do good, you receive good; if you do bad, you receive bad; therefore, you should do good and not do bad. This is a conventional way of talking.

But as one continues to practice, the understanding of Dhamma increases, and one is more aware of the true nature of things. Then, the idea of receiving good or receiving bad no longer makes sense. At that stage, there's no longer a question of doing good or doing bad. One acts on opportunities to do good, but the motivation is not based on the idea that anyone's going to receive anything for it. And one has no inclination to do bad things, because evil only has an attractive quality when there is the basic delusion of self. When that self-delusion is relinquished, then there are no problems left. There's the doing of good, but it's done because that's what's right, what's appropriate. It's not done for personal gain or benefit.

Question: So are you saying that, in the wise person, the goodness is just natural? There's no feeling that you have to do good—it's just a natural response to situations?

Answer: Yes, this natural response is in contrast to the impulsiveness that comes from ignorance. Without wisdom, we have impulses that we either follow or suppress. With wisdom, there's the spontaneity of responding to life from a universal pure mind, rather than from a personal idea of somebody who has to be good because they'll be punished if they're bad.

6

Mind and the Universe

B ecause we are thinking beings, the Buddha emphasized thinking in the right way. We can think in the wrong way about
ourselves and the universe, and we do this when we are
depressed and frightened. Once we start thinking in the right way, however, our fears, anxieties, and problems can dissolve. The important thing
in the Buddha's teaching is to establish our thinking on Right View.

Thinking of Ourselves Personally

Reflecting on my experience in the contemplative life, I would say that
wrong thinking is based on a view in which we are a self that is permanently separated from everything else. It is a view in which we think
that we are this person here, somehow cast forth into the universe and
conditioned by it, a helpless victim of circumstances. How many times
have you thought or heard other people comment, "What did I do to
deserve this? Why me? Why do these things have to happen to me?"
And how often do you find people wondering why they feel so lonely,
alienated, lost, or depressed? These are very common human experiences, aren't they? We often experience a feeling of isolation, separation,
and loneliness, a sense of being lost in a universal system that doesn't care
about us, that is impersonal, unloving, and unfair. When we judge the
experiences of our own lives from the position of permanent or absolute
separation from everything else, then of course the result is alienation,
fear, and anxiety. And our thoughts will stem from those feelings. The

way in which we perceive the world will be fraught with an attitude arising from that fear and anxiety.

The anxiety is justified, in a way. We are sensitive beings; we are vulnerable; these bodies can experience the most horrendous pain and discomfort, as we all know. We are all frightened that someday we might
get some terrible disease or be maimed or scarred. What we attach to,
what we depend on, what we like, can easily be changed to something
that we don't like. We can be separated from what we love, suddenly and
at any time. So, in one way, just because we are born in a human form,
with the ability to think about ourselves, our thoughts can cause us anxiety and worry.

We can take the human form very personally, as if all that we are is
just this body. We can think, "I'm this person whose personality has
been conditioned by life, by the family I was born into, by my education
or the lack of it, by the class I was born into." We can attach to and
identify with all the suggestions we have received throughout our life
about whether we are good or worthless, better than others or worse
than others. Because we can conceive of ourselves as being "something,"
we can attach to that concept and hold onto it for a lifetime. If we have
this wrong idea, then we are likely to live a whole lifetime thinking about
ourselves in the wrong way—and that certainly can be very painful.

We tend to react to life personally, and we can be hurt very easily just
by what other people say about us. If you say to me, "I don't like the way
you look," then I can feel hurt or wounded. We can spend a lifetime
resenting and being jealous of those who seem to have more privilege or
wealth than we do. Envy and jealousy are common human problems all
over the world. Now, if we couldn't think about ourselves, if we couldn't
view ourselves as a separate entity, then we wouldn't feel jealous, would
we? Jealousy definitely comes from the ability to think about ourselves.
We can think, "What did he do to deserve all those privileges? Why
can't I have the same?"

These are mental conditions, mental formations, that change, arise,
and cease. In Buddhism, we distinguish between the mind itself and
such mental formations. We define mental formations as the conditions
of the mind that arise and cease. Examples are the feelings, perceptions,

concepts, and sensory consciousness. The universe comprises everything that we can perceive and conceive of, so the universe itself comes under the category of mental formations.

Subject and Object

Of course we can also see the universe in a scientific way, as an object. Looking out into a starry night, we can contemplate the universe as if it were something out there, something separate from ourselves. We might also perceive the universe as though we were a part of it; but speaking for myself, I never used to perceive it in that way. Before I started meditating, the universe was something separate from me, and that separation was always a source of suffering because it left me feeling out of touch. If that sort of relationship with the universe is all we ever have, then ours is a rather pathetic life, and we never really understand it. We never really awaken to the mystery, vastness, and wonder of the universe. All we can do is try to live for the welfare of this particular body. We can spend our whole life trying to live in a safe place and not be hurt by anyone.

Consider this problem of separation between ourselves as a subject and the universe as an object. We are conscious beings; consciousness is the ability to be a subject that knows an object. But if the subjective aspect of consciousness gets distorted by views, prejudices, and biases, then we tend to misperceive the object. This happens whenever we grasp an idea and apply it generally—we form fixed views, prejudices, and biases. So if we perceive some other person as bad, then we see them as bad in a kind of continuous way. Whenever that person, name, or appearance arises in consciousness, the association of "bad" goes along with it. Thus, we can make ourselves insensitive by grasping views and opinions about ourselves and others. We lose our sensitivity, and therefore are not awake; we are just reacting.

We can live our whole life simply reacting—with racial prejudice, for instance. People don't contemplate and see that race itself is a subjective perception of the mind, so they form opinions about one race's being better than another, or about social classes, men and women, nations and religions. Through not really examining the nature of thought and its limitations, we can get caught up in our own thinking. However, instead of reacting from unexamined views and opinions, we can contemplate thought, because thought arises and ceases.

Thinking is impermanent. It moves quickly, producing one thought after another. We are conditioned to think by association: as one thought ceases, it gives rise to another, forming an endless stream. We can get caught up in these thoughts, judging them or identifying with them. Or we can begin to contemplate thought itself as impermanent, as something that comes and goes in our minds, whether it is rational or irrational, intelligent or stupid, true or false. We can contemplate it as thought, as that which arises and ceases, rather than trying to think about thinking, or to analyze the motivation for our thought. Doing that sort of analysis tends to reinforce our sense of being an isolated, separate self with personality.

Personality as the Subject

What I mean by personality includes the views, opinions, memories, and all that is conditioned into the mind from life experience. Personality is a condition, not ultimately true, or real; it's not the real subject. Instead, it's an object to be investigated.

If we allow our personality, with its views and biases, to be the subject of our consciousness, we experience reality in terms of that personality. Because the personality can take any form, we can be elated or depressed—we can feel successful or feel like a failure. We live in a culture that very much emphasizes personality as being oneself. To have a personality, to be a person, to have rights as a person, to be a man or a woman, to belong to a group or class or family or nation or club—all of these are taken very personally. Even what is impersonal—the natural functions of our human body that have nothing to do with personality—we make personal. We don't like to be identified with the functions of the body, unless they are nice or pleasant. Many people regard the aging process of the body, sickness, and pain in a very personal way. Natural drives such as hunger and sexuality—even the most instinctual, impersonal functions of a human body—are interpreted in this very personal way. They are judged as being good or bad, allowable or unwanted, refined or coarse.

So that's the personality view. If we are feeling good, we are happy; if we are not feeling good, we are unhappy. Any success that comes to this being is personal, and any failure is also personal. Any praise is taken personally, or any criticism; so there is going to be pleasure with praise and anguish with criticism. But when pleasure and pain, praise and blame, are seen from the viewpoint of the subject who is aware—rather than the viewpoint of a person—this is the awakened mind.

Awareness as the Subject

When we contemplate more and more, we are making pure awareness the subject of consciousness. In this pure awareness, conditions are seen simply as conditions, rather than being judged and reacted to from the personality viewpoint. So the Buddha emphasized the practice of mindfulness, in which we give up attachment, in which we are awake to the way things are, without judgment. If we are mindful, then we are not judging something; we are just observing it. We can even observe our own reactions.

Mindfulness is coupled with wisdom, the ability to contemplate the way things are. For this we can make use of the teachings of the Buddha as skillful means to help us watch and observe. And when there is mindfulness and wisdom, the subject of the mind is not personal anymore. The subject is not mine or ours, it does not have a name, it's not a man or a woman. All the personal conditions and attachments cease in it. You see the cessation, the ending of personality, but there is still awareness and the ability to reflect wisely on the way things are in this sensory realm. In the awakened mind, pain and pleasure are just the way things are. When there is reflective wisdom, we are not picking and choosing— pain and pleasure are of equal value. They're seen for what they are.

The senses always operate in a dualistic way. We, as subjects, see things as objects. Having eyes means that we are going to see whatever is in front of them; we're going to be conscious of it, whether it's the most beautiful thing or the most hideous. This applies to all the sense organs. The awakened mind is not shutting out this sensitivity, nor is it just reacting out of habit and conditions. It is responsive, and finds suitable responses to the experiences that arise. One can find a spontaneity that is only possible when the mind is not just reacting, because reactions are impulsive. Reaction is the following of impulses, but spontaneity comes from the purity of being awake, from mindfulness and wisdom. It no longer has anything to do with being a person, a type, or a character. Any being who is awake has the ability to respond appropriately to what is happening.

The Universe of the Mind

Contrast the perception of the universe with the perception of this human form. When you think about yourself as a person, it's rather frightening because the universe seems vast and endless according to our perceptions. We talk about aeons of time and vast distances measured in light-years, which we can't imagine; scientists talk about stars being near, when they are billions of miles away. But within this sensual human form, we can reflect on the universe from the actual sensory impingement we receive from it.

We can speculate about being influenced by the planets and forces from outer space; it's certainly possible. People question, "How could Pluto be affecting my life?" But why couldn't it be affecting our lives? We are part of the same universal system, and it seems fully possible that everything is affecting everything. I wouldn't exclude Pluto and Neptune from that, but I don't know how, or exactly in what way, they might affect us. Or maybe we're influencing Pluto; that's possible too. But then it gets too complicated, doesn't it?

If we reflect that everything is affecting everything, this gives us a sense of the totality and the wholeness of the universal system that we are very much involved with and can witness as a human being. However, we have to accept the limitation of being a separate individual. The universe we contemplate is the universe of the mind with its perceptions of pleasure and pain, beauty and ugliness. We can realize that the whole universe is about sensitivity and forces and powers and energy. We can see that, no matter how vast and powerful the forms in the universe might be, they have the characteristics of beginning and ending, birth and death, expansion and contraction. And we can contemplate the universe in seemingly insignificant experiences, such as breathing, the feeling of the body, or an emotion of anguish or desire.

Within the limitations of the human form, we can't understand the nature of existence from the universal position of an All-Seeing God, with a macrocosmic view. What we can do is observe existence close-up, without judgment. We have to work from the microcosmic view of this mind, even if the view seems incredibly personal, stupid, or irrational.

That's what I mean by contemplating the microcosm. We can observe the tendency in ourselves to grasp or reject, to be attracted or repelled. We can see the strong desire in our minds to become something else, to seek something, to wait for the next thing. We get caught up in this desire to become something because we aren't abiding in the way things are. We experience praise and blame, success and failure, pleasure and pain, sickness and death as personal. Everything seems personal, and everything seems painful. But, when seen from the awakened mind, things are as they are, and this point of view is the way out of suffering.

Trust in the Dhamma

I feel a tremendous trust now. I feel confidence in what we call the Dhamma—in the Way Things Are—because it's no longer important what happens to me, to this creature here. It's no longer a worry. Whatever happens—the best, the worst, praise, blame, success, failure, leukemia, or robust good health till the age of ninety-five and a peaceful death as one sits down in meditation—feel confident that it's all right the way it is. See it as Dhamma, rather than interpreting it and giving it a personal quality.

In Buddhism, we often talk about courage and fearlessness. Whenever we take the personal view, we are frightened, and we do cowardly things. We think, "I am going to suffer. What I love is going to be taken away from me. I'll lose my health, be an invalid, feel pain. Nobody will love me, and I'll be left alone. Life will be horrible. I'll be lost, alone, unloved, in pain, old and sick, poor me!" That's a lot to be frightened of, isn't it? But when these fears are seen as Dhamma, then even the worst is bearable. We realize that this is not a permanent person or position that we are involved in. This is a transition from birth to death within the human form. And what we have, as human beings, is the opportunity to awaken between birth and death.

In the awakened mind, there is no fear. There is knowing, there is clarity, and it's not personal. It's not mine; it's not yours. When all things cease, what remains is clarity, intelligence, brightness. We can call that "the true subject." When people ask, "But what is my true nature?" I answer, "It's peaceful, intelligent, calm, and bright. It's deathlessness—but don't take that personally."

Question: Could you describe further the nature of the pure mind?

Answer: Well, this is where the Buddha was very careful, because when you're trying to describe the indescribable, or define the indefinable, or limit the unlimited, you can get yourself into a lot of delusion. The only thing I can say is that, as you let go of things more and more, and as you realize that all that arises ceases, you realize the cessation of things—and then you realize the unconditioned.

There's the conditioned and the unconditioned, the created and the uncreated. You can't conceive of the uncreated. You have a word but there's no perception for it. There's no kind of symbol that one can grasp. You can have a doctrine about it, so religions tend to state metaphysical doctrines that people believe in. However, since the Buddhist teaching is a non-doctrinal teaching in which you're encouraged to find things out for yourself, you are left without any metaphysical doctrine, and this absence of doctrine is conducive to true realization. What realization brings is the understanding that the conditioned realm only arises and ceases. It is not eternal, and it is not infinite. It's only a movement in the universal.

Terminology and concepts for this realization can be very misleading. We've had dialogues with Christians, and I notice Christian meditators now are moving more toward the Buddhist position and saying quite untraditional things like, "God is nothing or no-thing." Buddhists understand that "no-thing" is probably a fairly accurate description. In contrast, trinitarian Christianity usually gives conditioned attributes for perceiving God as a Father, Son, or Holy Spirit. Mystical Christianity transcends this trinitarian view and talks about mystery, or not knowing. Christian mystics don't have the same psychological vocabulary that we do in Buddhism, so they tend to put it in a different way. But if you get beyond the terminology, you'll find that they describe the experience of the mind that is free from a self-view—and from a binding to the conditioned world. Hinduism and Islam have this in some form as well. So one sees the potential in all religions to point beyond themselves.

The danger is always in attachment to the conventions. Even with Buddhism, as beautiful and clear a teaching as it is, not many Buddhists use it to be enlightened. They tend to attach to a certain part of the teaching. However, at present, I think there's more potential for awakening to the truth, which isn't just Buddhist, but is beyond all conventions.

There's a lot of really clear thinking going on now among human beings, and it's quite wonderful. There is a mental clarity and use of wisdom that is happening in different places on the planet. No matter how gloomy and pessimistic the newspapers sometimes are about the state of the world, I can't help but feel more optimistic. I can see that it is changing. In just my own lifetime, there's been a remarkable change in the development of a spiritual understanding and wisdom.

$$7$$

Nibbāna

We use the word "*nibbāna*" for the goal of our meditation, which is to realize non-attachment. As unenlightened human beings, we tend to attach to things out of ignorance, out of not understanding things properly. We're always attaching and grasping at everything; however, when we realize non-attachment, we experience *nibbāna*. Sometimes *nibbāna* is translated as "extinction," so it sounds rather forbidding, like annihilation. But it does not require that we annihilate things, only that we let go of our attachment to them.

Nibbāna refers to the realization human beings have when they are not grasping anything. In that realization of non-grasping, one experiences a connection. One is in alignment with the divine because, when there is non-grasping, there is the real experience of compassion. One feels compassion, joyfulness, happiness, and serenity, not because of any personal attainment or achievement, but because there is nobody there. There is no grasping of the body as self; there is no grasping of views or opinions or feelings or anything else; there is simply non-grasping. When you realize non-grasping, you experience true ease, peacefulness, and bliss. But this state of happiness is not the usual one for human beings. We must train the mind and heart to realize it.

Awareness Based on Knowing

If you learn to calm the mind, you begin to sense a continuous awareness that is firm, stable, and constant. It is based on simply knowing and being alert, rather than on concepts, ideas, views, and emotions, which come and go. You begin to know that this is the way it is. This sense of knowing is what people sometimes describe as "suchness" or "as-is-ness," and it's based in the moment as it is now. Consider what happens to your mind when I say, "This is the way it is now." I'm not telling you how it is, or how you should see it or feel it. I'm not telling you what you should be experiencing. I'm not pointing to any object or anything at all, or describing the experience in any way. I'm just saying, "This is the way it is now, the suchness, as it is now." When I use this thought, I open the mind; I feel more with the moment, receptive to what's happening, rather than looking for something to fix on. I'm not trying to describe the moment, but just open to it. So the mind can go quite empty; the thought process stops, and the mind opens. This is the way it is. With this sense of awareness, we can reflect on the way it is at this time: there's the breathing, there's a body here, there are feelings in the body. There's silence, the time is now, the place is here—this is the way it is.

When we investigate the way things are, rather than using concepts and theories, we use our ability to perceive in order to point beyond perception—to awareness itself. For the most part, our minds aren't trained to do this. Normally, we're trained to operate from assumptions, theories, and positions. We may believe in a God, and make the basic assumption that there is a creator God who made us, and then from that follows all the other assumptions we make. It's not that such a doctrine is wrong, but if we operate from an assumption, we don't ever really witness and know how things are. We just believe and accept what other people tell us.

When the Buddha taught the Four Noble Truths, he was teaching human beings to open the mind. He was helping us to be aware of nature as it operates, not through any scientific or psychological theory or philosophical position, but from attention to the way things happen to be. We're using what we have. We're not trying to create ideas and interesting theories about the way things are, but actually to observe them, from the most obvious conditions that we generally take for granted.

The mind creates lots of interesting theories. For example, we talk about gender differences: men are this way, women are that way. We're used to speaking in these conceptual terms, but actually, these differences are based on qualities that are changing, not fixed or permanent. Even though our bodies are either male or female, these conditions are subject to all other conditions. If we don't witness and observe this dependency on conditions, we tend to take fixed positions as men, women, Englishmen, or Americans—as if these were ultimate truths. What we see are only conventional realities, but we can live our lives operating on the assumption that these are the real things. People talk about the "real world," but the real world that they talk about is not real; it is only conventional appearance. It's the way it seems to be, according to the way one has been conditioned to perceive it.

Seeing the True Nature of Conditions

The Buddha's teaching points to the fact that all conditions are impermanent (P. *sabbe sankhārā aniccā*). By the word "condition" (P. *sankhārā*), we mean a formation of the mind, such as a thought or opinion.

Men and women are conditions. Similarly, Jews and Gentiles, Buddhists and Christians, Asians and Europeans, Africans, the working class, the middle class, the upper class—all these are only formations that go through the mind. They aren't absolutes. They are merely conventions that are useful for communication. We must use these conventions, but we must also realize that they are only conventions—not absolutes. In this way, our minds are no longer fixed in our views or opinions. Views and opinions are seen simply as conditions that arise and cease in the mind, because that's what they really are. All conditions are impermanent; they arise and cease.

The Buddha's teaching also points to the fact that all things are not self (P. *sabbe dhammā anattā*). This is a little more advanced, but as we meditate more and more and as we see into the nature of things, it becomes clearer that all things are not self. The need to identify with, and belong to, some condition or some position, falls away. We're no longer looking for ourselves or trying to find names for ourselves, or trying to identify ourselves with anything whatsoever. This is the freedom, the liberation from attachment to conditions that leads to *nibbāna.*

As we continue to practice, we become more aware of the truth of the way it is. This truth, or Dhamma, becomes more and more meaningful to us. It becomes very useful as a reflection, because Dhamma includes everything, both the conditioned and the unconditioned, the mortal and the immortal. When we understand Dhamma, we don't take sides: we're not rejecting mortality by holding onto a concept of immortality. However, as we free ourselves from attachment to mortality, then of course what's left is immortality. So a wise person recognizes the nature of conventional reality as impermanent, unsatisfactory, and not self, (the three characteristics of all conditioned phenomena) and is aware enough to know when there's no attachment to conditions.

Saṁsāra is the state of being attached and suffering. In this state, we say things like, "I wish I didn't think like that. I wish those problems would go away. I don't want this. I'm afraid of that. I don't like this. I shouldn't be this way. You shouldn't be that way." That's *saṁsāra.* All those screaming, possessive, frightened, greedy little voices. When you're attached to all that, it's *saṁsāra. Saṁsāra* is the realm of suffering. *Nibbāna* is the realm of freedom from suffering through non-attachment. When we recognize whatever happens in our minds, whether it's negative or positive, critical or affirmative, simply as conditions, this is the Buddha-mind, this is *nibbāna.*

Inclining toward Deathlessness

When we say "practicing the Dhamma," what do we mean? The practice is the constant reflection and reminder of the way things are, the opening of the mind to the way it is. Now if I come into this room with a prejudice of some sort, perhaps through anger, I'm no longer fully capable of understanding the way things are. I'm blinded and obsessed. But if I'm aware that I'm really angry and that there's a very strong feeling overwhelming me, even if I'm just aware of that much, then at that moment I've recognized it as a condition. So the force of attachment is diminished; there's a slight bit of non-attachment. And even if I'm carried away again, as soon as I realize I've been carried away, there's another breaking of the cycle. In other words, the cycle that's there is not being reinforced; it's being weakened. So the force of my anger weakens and diminishes the more I reflect on it.

If we sincerely try to detach, even if it's just a little bit, then we become less and less enslaved to appearances, to the force of habit, to the cycle of birth and death, to *saṁsāra*. Then we're inclining toward the deathlessness, toward the realization of *nibbāna*. But the more we are committed to the obsessions of the mind, and allow ourselves to be carried away and then taken over by them, the more we're reinforcing *saṁsāra*.

When we're carried away, it's as if we were whirled around and around, until we suddenly realize that we've been caught in the birth and death cycle. That point of realization is the inclination toward deathlessness, and that point of mindfulness and comprehension—even if it's just a flash—is an experience of *nibbāna*. Of course, the passion might be so strong that it overwhelms us again and we get carried away with guilt, frustration, discouragement, annoyance, or whatever it is. It goes on and on and on until suddenly we're aware once more, and we have another experience of freedom. When we're overwhelmed, the problem is that we believe the emotion, along with all the subsequent conditions. And the problem is compounded by our not wanting the emotion and the guilt about it—the whole cycle.

Over the years, it can seem that we don't achieve anything or even change all that much. But then, we realize that, in situations when we're overwhelmed, we can somehow get through them a little bit better. We find that we're not so caught up, blinded, and utterly helpless in the face of these passions or fears. Gradually, we see that *saṁsāra*, or sensory consciousness, is a movement, a vibration, a changing thing with no substance and no eternal or permanent essence. There's no way we can capture it and say, "This is it," but we can observe it.

We begin to see that everything is as it is. It has no name other than the name we give it. It is we who call it something; we give it a value. We say this thing is good, or it's bad, but in itself, the thing is only as it is.

It's not absolute; it's just as it is. People are just as they are. We can give them names, and we can describe them. We can decide whether we like them or don't like them, whether we are attracted to them or repelled by them. That's something we add or project onto the moment because of our habits, fears, and desires. That's why it is very important to contemplate the way things are in the moment. It's through this experience that we can be aware of what we project onto it.

This body is just this way. Having been born and lived a number of years, it's this way. But now, I can begin to cogitate about it —I don't like it, I like it, I wish it would look different, younger, etc. I can create all kinds of views and opinions about the body, but it's just the way it is. It feels this way; it looks that way. This is the suchness. It doesn't mean we're not aware of the body's beauty or its ugliness; it just means we're not making anything, creating anything, out of it. We can be aware of an imperfection without making any problem about it. In other words, the mind becomes an embracing mind.

The Way out of Suffering

We can find the way out of suffering by being completely with life as it's happening, by embracing life. We cannot find the way by running from everything in order to protect and defend ourselves from all possible forms of danger and insecurity. That's what people often think monks are doing—that we're running away from life because we can't face the real world. But in fact, the experience is one of opening the mind to embrace the whole. Through practice, we begin to feel at ease in just being with the way things are, rather than always having to attach to them, hold onto them, reject them, or ignore them. We begin to feel a sense of ease and peacefulness through just being with life as it is, rather than having everything figured out from particular viewpoints.

For example, I could ask, "What would you do if you were in a little room with an angry, deadly poisonous snake?" You could speculate about whether you should kill the snake to protect yourself. If you've taken a Buddhist vow not to harm living creatures, you might feel you shouldn't kill the snake. You could go back and forth about this hypothetical case from various viewpoints. But what actually happens, of course, in a crisis like this, is that there's no time to ponder what to do: you have to trust in your instinct. You can't figure it out ahead of time.

I've been asked to speculate about whether I'd kill a maniac who was about to attack my mother. If I were a conscientious objector, then my viewpoint might require me to say, "Well, I'd just pray." And people would say, "You mean you'd just let that man stab your sweet little old mother?" But if a maniac attacked my mother, and I was around, I trust that the wisdom of the moment would direct me to do the right thing. I can't say what I'd do because I don't know all the things that would be affecting that moment. Maybe at that time my mother would have a heart attack and just die anyway, or maybe the maniac would have an epileptic fit. Or maybe the maniac would suddenly think, "I can't harm this sweet little old lady. Her son over there is a pacifist, and he can't protect her." Or maybe my mother would have become a karate expert and would give him a chop. Or the police would come. Who knows what could happen—the telephone might ring or the chandelier might fall on his head—that's fair enough if you're speculating, isn't it? We can go on imagining all the possible things that might happen in a moment, but all we can say is that we don't know. Right now, we don't know what we'd do because none of those conditions are present. But we can know the way it is now, can't we? We can be open to the present moment without reference to a particular viewpoint.

The Experience of Nibbāna

In many circles, nibbāna (Skt. nirvāna) is the common word for anything ecstatic or heaven-like, but actually, it means "not bound to the conditions of birth and death." It refers to the experience of non-attachment. When we are really aware, there's no need, no inclination, to identify with the body or the conditions of mind—these are as they are. This is not a rejection or annihilation of the human body or mental conditions, but it's a way of seeing them as they are. They arise and cease; they begin and end.

That clarity of observation, that awareness of the mind—the realization of *nibbāna*—is not all that far away. It's not something that's beyond anyone's capabilities. If you assume you can't do it, then of course you tend to operate from that basic assumption, so you never do. But the Buddha said very definitely that this is a teaching for human beings, people with moral responsibility; intelligent beings. So, are you one of these? If you aren't, then maybe you'd better reform—you don't have to be a rascal.

So *nibbāna* is not a kind of ethereal state out in the sky, or in outer space, or in the next life. The Buddha always pointed to the way things are now, to what actually can be known and realized by each one of us within our limitations as human beings, at this time and this place. This is where your reflection and looking into the nature of things needs to be developed, so that you can really begin to know this truth, rather than just speculate about it—or guess, or believe, or disbelieve. You can begin to wisely reflect and penetrate, experiencing freedom by not attaching to things.

Question: How would you describe enlightenment?

Answer: Enlightenment is nothing more than growing up, being a mature being. The perfection of the human *kamma* is enlightenment. This means becoming mature, being responsible and balanced, being a moral and wise human being who is no longer looking for "someone to love me."

Many of us can't find love in someone else, so we want God to love us. We say, "I believe in a god that loves me. Nobody else does, but God loves me." But that's immature—to want love from out there—from someone else. The enlightened being doesn't need to be loved by God or anyone. It's nice to be loved by others, but it's not necessary.

Enlightenment is practical; it's something each one of us can realize. We are all capable of moving into the position of being awake. And when we're awake and balanced and wise, we can love. That is the maturing of the human being. When there is wisdom, one naturally relates to others with love. Love is wisdom's natural radiance.

PART II
Awakening the Mind

And gladness springs up within him on his realizing that, and joy arises to him thus gladdened, and so rejoicing, all his frame becomes at ease, and being thus at ease he is filled with a sense of peace, and in that peace his heart is stayed.

Dīgha Nikāya
Sāmaññaphala Sutta, 73

8

Introduction to Meditation

The important thing in meditation is attitude, rather than technique or tradition. The right attitude is most important. Even if you have the best teacher with the best tradition and the best methods, if your attitude isn't right, it won't work.

Many people meditate with an attitude of gaining, attaining, or achieving. It's not surprising, because our worldly attitude is based on achievement. We are conditioned by our education and society to see life as something we must use in order to attain or become something. On a worldly level, this is the way it is. We have to go to school in order to learn to read and write. We have to do all kinds of things in order to become something or to attain something, but enlightenment (*nibbāna*) is not something that we ever attain or achieve. This is a difficult thing to comprehend with the intellect, because the intellect is conditioned to think in terms of gaining.

Practicing without Gain

The words "Dhamma" and "*nibbāna*" are untranslatable because they cannot be explained conceptually: they are realizations rather than things. The best we can do in English is to use a term like "ultimate reality." Dhamma and *nibbāna* are what we realize rather than something we attain or achieve.

When we are meditating, our intention is to incline toward *nibbāna* rather than toward attaining a higher state of consciousness. There are various meditation techniques in which we can achieve higher levels of consciousness, but for *nibbāna* there are no stages, there are no levels, there's no attainment. There's no development or progress because it's a realization rather than an attainment.

The problem human beings have with meditation is their worldly mind. The worldly mind is always looking for something. Even if one meditates for years, there's still a great desire in the mind to find out "Who am I? What am I? What is the purpose of my life?" But the Buddha was not trying to tell us the purpose of life. Instead, he tried to give us guidance to full realization. Therefore, in his basic teaching of the Four Noble Truths, he pointed to everything that is not self, rather than make any statement about what we are or what our true nature is. Even if he had told us exactly what we are, we still wouldn't really know until we had meditated and found out for ourselves.

Everything That Is Not Self

The Buddha pointed to everything that is not self. In Pali, this "everything" is referred to as the five *khandhas*, translated as the five heaps, or the five aggregates. These are listed as: physical form, feeling, perception, volition (or mental formations), and sense consciousness. These are what we are not—and this "not being anything" is what we mean by *anattā*, or non-self. Everything that you can perceive and conceive, know through the senses, or think with the mind—everything mental and physical that has a beginning and an end, that arises and passes away—is included in the five heaps. The five aggregates include the whole universe that we perceive and conceive through our senses.

The five aggregates include our bodies. These human bodies are products of the earth, and their nature is to rely on all the things that the earth produces. We have to eat what comes from the earth, and when these bodies die, the elements of earth, water, fire, and air return to the earth again. Seeing our bodies as part of a larger process is a way of recognizing *anattā*, a way of seeing that these bodies are not self.

In conventional reality, of course, the body is very much our "self." When I talk about myself, I am talking about this body; I am not talking about anything else. But when we investigate and reflect, we begin to comprehend the truth of *anattā* as an actual experience. We are no longer deluded into thinking that we actually are our body, feelings, perceptions, volition, and sense consciousness. We know what is not ourself, fully and completely, without any doubt remaining. This is complete enlightenment, and this is what our meditation is about.

The Conditioned and the Unconditioned

The teaching of the Buddha is a very simple teaching, because it comprehends things in terms of the conditioned and the unconditioned. Conditioned phenomena are those which arise and pass away. They include everything that we perceive and know through our senses, through the body, feelings, thoughts, and memories. They are conditions; they begin and they end. The Pali term for the conditioned is *sankhāra*. *Sankhāra* includes all that arises and passes away, whether it is mental or physical. We are not quibbling about whether it is out there or in here, whether something arises and passes away in an instant or in an aeon. It does not make any difference as far as this way of meditating goes, because the conditioned includes all time-bound things.

The unconditioned is something that most people never realize because they are mesmerized by conditioned phenomena. To realize the unconditioned we have to let go of our constant attachment to conditioned phenomena.

The unconditioned is like the space in a room. When you come into a room, do you notice the space, or is your attention drawn to the objects in the room? You see the walls, the windows, the people, the furniture, the colors, and the decorations. But the space in the room is not noticeable, even though it is there all the time. And when we're busy watching all the people and the objects in the room, we don't notice the space at all. It is only when we let go of thinking, talking, considering, and imagining, that we become aware and we notice the space in the room. When we attend to it, we see that space is peaceful and boundless. Even the walls of the room do not limit space.

It's the same with the mind. The mind is unlimited and has no boundaries; it can contain everything. Yet we bind ourselves to the limited conditions of the mind—our ideas, views, and opinions. There is room enough in space for every theory, opinion, and view; they all arise and pass away, and there is no permanent condition. So there is room enough for everybody and everything, for every religion, every political view, every thought, every type of human being. And yet, humanity always wants to control and limit and say: "Only these we allow, and those do not have any right to be here." Trying to possess and hold on, we bind ourselves to conditions, which always take us to death and despair.

Whatever we hope and expect will cause us to feel disillusionment and despair, if we attach to it. This is because whatever we attach to arises and has to pass away. There is nothing that arises which keeps on arising; it can only arise for so long, and then it passes away. So when you bind yourself to any condition that is arising, it can only take you along with it as it passes away. When you attach to anything that is arising, such as your own physical body or any condition in nature, it will take you to death. And so death is the end of that which was born, and despair is the other side of hope and expectation.

As soon as anything becomes unpleasant or unsatisfactory, we tend to jump into some other condition, into something that is arising. This makes life a constant search for pleasure, romance, and adventure. People are always running after that which is interesting or fascinating and running away from the opposite. We run from boredom, despair, old age, sickness, and death because these are conditions that we do not want to be with. We want to get away from them, forget them, not notice them.

But in meditation, the attitude is to be infinitely patient with conditions, even when they become unpleasant or boring. If we're always running off to find something more interesting, we just keep going round in circles. This is called the cycle of *saṁsāra*.

Meditating on the Ordinary

When we notice that the conditions of body and mind are just the way conditions are, it's a simple recognition. It's not an analysis, and it's not anything special. It's just a bare recognition, a direct knowing that whatever arises passes away. Knowing in this way demands a certain amount of patience; otherwise, as soon as any fear, anger, or unpleasantness arises, we will run away from it. So meditation is also the ability to endure, and bear with, the unpleasant. We don't seek it out; we are not ascetics looking for painful things to endure so that we can prove ourselves. We're simply recognizing the way it is right now.

The Buddha established his meditation on that which is ordinary, rather than on that which is extraordinary. For example, one technique of Buddhist meditation is mindfulness of the breath (P. *ānāpānasati*), which is meditation through attention to normal breathing. There are meditations on sitting, standing, walking, and lying down, which are also very ordinary—even boring. With meditation on these ordinary conditions, what is required is an attitude of infinite patience; we make all the time in the world to be with one inhalation and one exhalation. There's nothing else to do except to be with what is—with the body sitting down, the body standing up, the body walking, the body lying down.

That's a mental state very different from the one we are accustomed to, isn't it? When we are sitting down, we normally do not notice sitting. We might sit and collapse out of exhaustion, or we might sit and read, sit and smoke, sit and eat, or sit and talk. We're always doing something while we're sitting. And it's much the same with the other postures. When we lie down, we fall asleep heedlessly. We walk heedlessly, stand heedlessly, and sit heedlessly, so we never really see what is now and what is immediate. We are always thinking about what we have to do now in order to get what we want in the future, and that is endless. Even when you get what you want in the future, you find it only satisfies you temporarily, and then you start thinking of something else you have to have.

Looking at the Movement of Desire

I remember, when I was a little boy I saw a toy, and I told my mother, "If you buy me that toy, I promise I will never ask for anything ever again." I really believed that full satisfaction could be gained from own-ing that toy! So she went and bought the toy and gave it to me. I think I played with it a little while and set it aside, and then I found something else that I wanted. But I remember how thoroughly convinced I was that, if she would give me that one thing, my desires would be satisfied forever—and I remember that I was not satisfied. Even at that young age, this realization made an impression because I can still remember the lesson: even getting what I wanted was disappointing because then I had to start looking for something else.

In meditation, we are looking at the movement of desire, but we are not passing judgment against desire. Some people think that Buddhists are all against desire, but the Buddha's teaching is not an annihilation-ist teaching—it is an awakening. Desire is not something that we reject, or try to annihilate. We reflect on it and understand that it is a condi-tion in nature.

There are desires that are good and desires that are bad. Desires to kill, hurt others, and steal are considered bad desires; all of us have bad desires at times. And then, there are good desires that make us want to help, be kind, or develop into good and wise beings. Whenever we recognize desire—whether it is good or bad—we are using wisdom. Only wisdom can see desire; desire cannot see wisdom. So when you are trying to find wisdom, just know desire. Watching the movement of desire lets us see its nature as a changing condition. And we see that it is not self.

Buddha-Wisdom

Buddha-wisdom is something that we use in our meditation, not some-thing we attain. It's a humbling kind of wisdom; it's not fantastic. It's the simple wisdom of knowing that whatever arises passes away and is not self. It is knowing that the desires going through our minds are just that—they are desires, and they are not us. Wisdom is living as men, women, monks, nuns, Buddhists, Christians, or whatever, using the conventional realities of gender, role, class, and so forth, but under-standing those realities as mere conventions. Wisdom lets us see that they are not ultimate truth, so that they do not delude us.

Buddha-wisdom is that which knows the conditioned as the conditioned and the unconditioned as the unconditioned. It's as simple as that. You just have to know two things: the conditioned and the unconditioned. When you are meditating, don't try to attain, but just open up to your intention for meditating. When you suddenly awaken to the fact that you are trying to get something out of it, that is a moment of enlightenment. With an open mind, you begin to see what is really happening. But if you sit for a year trying to become and attain, you will feel terribly disappointed at the end of it. You will have lost everything because, if you don't have the right attitude, you will not have the wisdom to learn from failure.

In our meditation, we learn from both successes and failures. People fail all the time. Mindfulness of the breath is one of the most frustrating meditation practices ever conceived because, if you try to get something out of it, it is not a very giving practice. You have to be patient. You have to learn from your successes and from your failures, until you no longer really care whether your experience is pleasant or unpleasant. Then both conditions can take you to enlightenment, to *nibbāna*.

Question: Is the appearance of light in meditation a hindrance or a good sign?

Answer: Well you see, it's not the appearance of light that is an obstacle. The problem is the grasping of it from a self-view. Light is a positive sign, really, but where the difficulty arises is in its interpretation. In meditation, when extraordinary things happen, we should simply observe them as impermanent. We reflect, "What arises ceases," rather than thinking, "Oh, I've seen the light, I'm pure, I've attained something."

The first year that I meditated in Nongkhai, I was in robes, but I didn't have a teacher. I was in a monastery, but I couldn't speak Thai, and nobody could speak English. I had just one book in English that I could use, and I was following this book very closely. It was basic Theravadan teaching and I found it very helpful, but I would go into fantastic states.

I'd see lights, and I'd feel full of bliss as I meditated. My interpretation of these experiences was that I had attained something. I remember thinking one time that I was a completely enlightened being, and I thought, "Well that didn't take very long. I thought it was going to take years of hard work, but only a few months in a monastery and here I am." I felt certain that I was enlightened.

After that period in an isolated monastery, I had to go to Bangkok. Traveling on the train and arriving in Bangkok, I found that the enlightened being totally collapsed, and there was this terribly confused American wandering around Bangkok. That was a great disappointment. I was expecting to radiate light all over Bangkok. Instead, I was radiating something else that wasn't very nice!

The following year, when I went to Ajahn Chah's monastery and I told him about these experiences, he just kept saying, "Well you know, it's attachment. Don't attach." And so I began to realize that I was very attached to those ecstatic experiences; I could see myself always trying to get to those states again. I thought that the experience of bliss was what I wanted. I remembered that first year and all those wonderful visions and experiences—and the second year I didn't get anything. It was just pain and depression and despair. So I'd do ascetic practices. I'd work very hard and do all the things that I remembered doing the first year, but it wouldn't work anymore. In fact, what I had to do was to just let go of remembering.

It wasn't that what happened the first year was deluded. It was just that my interpretation of it came from an egotistical position, and the memories were so pleasant that I wanted to have those same experiences again. I now realize that I had those blissful experiences in the first year because they were not called up from memory; they came on their own. I had never felt that way before or had those kinds of experiences, so they were totally new. They were just as they were. They weren't fabricated or created in my mind. But later, as I remembered them, the tendency was to try to create them in my mind again, and that didn't work.

I realized from that experience that lights and visions are not important in meditation. The important thing is to develop mindfulness, to accept more limitation, and to be with the flow of daily life—rather than seek ecstatic experiences. I changed my attitude when I went to Ajahn Chah. Instead of seeking ecstasies and the heights of religious experience, I developed an acceptance of daily life—of the heat and the mosquitoes.

With mindfulness and acceptance, you begin to see that the true light is your ability to be in alignment with wisdom. You realize that seeing things clearly in everyday life is the enlightened mind. It's not some kind of light flashing at you from the outside. It's being light yourself.

9

Mindfulness of the Breath

Mindfulness of the breath (P. *ānāpānasati*) is a basic meditation technique in which we concentrate on the sensation of our breath. For this practice, we must develop great patience. We must always be willing to begin again, because the mind repeatedly becomes distracted from the breath. The mind is not used to being tied down to one object; it's been taught to associate one thing with another, and it moves quickly from one association to the next. Using our ability to think in such clever ways, we tend to become very restless when we try to concentrate on just one object, like the breath. We can even become tense when we can't use our minds in the usual, associative way. So when we are doing *ānāpānasati*, we may feel a resistance or resentment.

If an animal has always lived in the wild and it is suddenly harnessed, it becomes angry and resists the things that are holding it down. Like any wild thing, an untrained mind lives on its own terms, following its instincts and habits; it is of little use to anyone else. However, when you train a wild horse, it becomes something that can help others. It's the same with our minds. If we just let them follow our habits, if we put no effort into our lives to tame the wild mind, then we are going to be like a wild creature—of no use to anyone, not even ourselves.

To tame the mind, we restrain it. We keep it focused on a single object. The breath is a handy object for meditation because the physiological function of breathing goes on, whether we concentrate on it or not. It is not something we create or imagine. It's something that is always going on naturally, so we can turn to it as an object of meditation at any time. If we concentrate on the rhythm of normal breathing, which is quite tranquilizing, we feel very calm and peaceful. But we tend to overlook our breath. Like anything ordinary, it is not something we pay attention to. The breath is not very exciting, so *ānāpānasati* is a subtle practice.

Ordinary Breath

We can become restless and averse to the breath because we always have the desire to get something. We want to find something that easily interests us, something we can focus on without much effort. If we find something interesting, such as exciting, rhythmic music, we absorb right into it. But the rhythm of normal breath isn't interesting or compelling. It's calming, and most beings aren't used to tranquillity; they are caught in their need to be excited and interested. In other words, most of us need something outside of ourselves to stimulate and excite us, and to engage our attention.

Just look around in a city; much of it is there to draw us in, to make us want to absorb into this or that. There are beautiful things, exotic foods, exciting entertainment; such things are easily available now. People like to take drugs because all they've got to do is swallow in order to be dazzled by an hallucination. It is not like *ānāpānasati*, where you're watching one inhalation and then one exhalation. It's not like spending half an hour noticing the beginning, the middle, and the end of each inhalation and exhalation.

The habit of desire begins because watching the breath doesn't seem to be very important or necessary. Most people think, "Why waste time doing that? What are you monks and nuns doing just sitting there? What are you doing for the Third World? What are you doing to help humanity? You're just selfish; you expect people to give you food while you just sit there and watch your breath. You are running away from the real world, aren't you?"

But what is the real world? And who's running away from what, and what is there to face? We find that what people call the "real world" is the world they believe in and are familiar with. That world is a condition of the mind. In meditation, one is recognizing and acknowledging the real world as it actually is, rather than believing in it or justifying it or trying to annihilate its problematic nature.

The real world operates on the same pattern of arising and passing as the inhalation and the exhalation. Inhalation conditions exhalation, and exhalation conditions inhalation. You can't have just exhalation or just inhalation. That is the condition of all phenomena—they arise and pass away. So in Buddhist practice we are acknowledging the way nature is, rather than trying to rationalize with ideas.

We're watching nature when we are watching our breath. If we concentrate on this one thing, it allows us to see the pattern of arising and passing that holds true for all conditioned phenomena in their infinite variety. Things of the conditioned world are constantly changing and are infinitely variable; they have different qualities, quantities, and positions in space. Our minds cannot handle such complexity, so we have to learn from simplicity. We study something as ordinary and seemingly insignificant as normal breathing.

Developing Patience

At first, the mind will just wander off the breath, so we try to develop patience. Once we are aware that the mind has wandered off the breath, we very gently go back to the breath again. If we get upset when the mind wanders, we'll feel discouraged and averse to the whole thing, and then we'll try to force the mind through will power. But we can only do that for a little while before the mind goes off somewhere else again.

The right attitude to *ānāpānasati* is being very, very patient. We must feel that we have all the time in the world just to watch one inhalation. There's no need to get anything out of it. We are training the mind the way a good mother trains a child. A good mother knows that if she gets angry with the child and beats it, the child will become terrified and neurotic. Therefore, if the child wanders off, she draws it back firmly, but without anger. Having that kind of patience, we are not just bashing away, getting upset because we can't get tranquil with *ānāpānasati*.

Instead, we become wise and patient by being that way with an insignificant thing like a breath.

We might wish to be like a Buddha image, sitting up on a high lotus throne, radiating light from all the pores of our body, being able to sit for hours in a beautiful lotus posture. That kind of showmanship in meditation is certainly attractive. But the humility of Buddhist meditation is that it is nothing special, and it's not very noticeable in worldly terms. It's not anything that anyone would be tempted to write about in the headline of a newspaper: "Venerable Sumedho had one mindful inhalation this morning at 8 o'clock!" But actually, that would be better news than most of what's in the headlines.

Being Patient with Boredom

With *ānāpānasati*, one aspect of the breath is no more pleasing than another, so we can reflect on it with a neutral feeling. We have preferences for more extreme kinds of experience: we like excitement, but we try to get away from boredom. Yet excitement takes us to boredom, because nothing can stay permanently exciting. Anything that is exciting is like an inhalation—it is finite. It can only be exciting for that span, and then it becomes boring. When it becomes boring, what do we do? Well, the average person looks for something else that might be exciting, like romance.

Stories throughout the ages have been written about romance, because it is exciting. But romance is also impermanent; it has its span—like the inhalation. After it reaches its peak, it loses its fire. What was once a very exciting relationship becomes boring and we think, "What took the magic out of our romance? Where did the magic go?" We think we would like that kind of magic again so we have to look for someone else because it can't happen again with the same person. So some people spend their whole lives going from one romance to another. It's not wise, is it!

Others look for excitement in adventure under dangerous conditions. They have to do something like walk over the North Pole or climb Mount Everest—something that ordinary people wouldn't dare to do. They can maintain that for a while, but then even that becomes boring.

Notice that this is the way nature is: you can't have excitement without boredom—one conditions the other. And that means you have to be patient when the excitement changes into boredom.

Being Patient with Disillusionment

Sometimes people come to monasteries when they are really inspired, and they say they want to dedicate their entire lives to the Dhamma. But they should watch out—anyone who is that high is going to be disillusioned and depressed in the not-too-distant future. Meditation is easy when you're fascinated and the teacher inspires you; but then as you meditate, it becomes monotonous and boring. At first, you might try to arrange your life in a way that makes more time for meditation, but later you might find yourself arranging things so that you have less time. Of course, there are always important things to do in life, but what has really happened is that meditation, which was once fascinating, has become boring. And we want to turn away from anything boring.

Monks and nuns who have spent any time in the order have gone through tremendous disillusionment and despair with meditation. But one of the advantages of being a monk or a nun is that you can't get out of it very easily. The commitment is a little more, so that when you really get fed up with the whole thing, you are more enduring. You have all the things that hold you together and help you to stay with it until you understand the "exhalation" side of life—the boredom, the disillusionment, and even the despair. From that perspective, you begin to have true insight, and you begin to understand the way out of suffering.

It's only if you are willing to endure through despair and disillusionment that you can really know. If you delude yourself into thinking, "I don't believe in this any more," if you go off and follow some other interesting method or religion, you'll have to repeat the same cycle over and over. You'll just be going from one guru to the next, and from one type of meditation to another. Life can be interesting and inspiring, you can be very enthusiastic—and then what happens? It becomes boring and dreary.

Now in meditation, if you are really serious about insight, you can notice that boredom likewise has its allotted span. It's not a permanent state, even though it seems permanent when you lose enthusiasm and confidence. But that's just the way it seems. When you are depressed and disillusioned, everything looks hopeless and you can't imagine being happy ever again. If you don't have the wisdom to understand depression, you judge according to the way things seem to be at that time. What we like seems to go by very quickly, and what we don't like seems to stay forever. But we can learn something from those perceptions. We can observe how things seem to be, and we can remain undeluded by the appearance of the sensory world that we experience.

We can only develop this wisdom through practice and by reflecting on the way things are in our own lives. We have to learn it—painfully— for ourselves, just the way we had to learn to walk by falling down. Babies can't walk right away. They have to learn to walk by crawling, by holding on to things, by pulling themselves up, by falling down, and by pulling themselves back up again. It's the same with meditation. You learn wisdom by observing ignorance—by making a mistake, reflecting on it, and keeping going.

If you think about it, you'll say, "I'll never be able to get anywhere." If you think about yourself too much, you'll think you're hopeless and that you can never do it. That's why it's a good thing little children don't think very much; if they did, they'd never learn to walk. When you are watching a child trying to walk, it looks hopeless, doesn't it? It's the same with meditation: sometimes it seems completely hopeless. But that's just the way it seems, if you think about it. So you just keep doing the meditation practice—especially when you are disillusioned and you have to put extra effort into it.

Training the Mind in Daily Life

There are periods in a monastery for meditation—in the morning and in the evening. In between, we have other duties, so our life has a certain order to it. But also, there are periods of time when there is nothing to do. At such times, I used to find myself trying to do something other than meditation. Reading books is a good activity; it's easy to absorb into a book. But I've trained myself to practice *ānāpānasati* at times when there is nothing on the schedule—even when I want to drink tea or chat or do anything but watch my breath. This is a way of composing and collecting oneself so that practice becomes integrated, rather than just a practice to do in strictly defined circumstances.

I've also found *ānāpānasati* to be very good for situations in which life becomes terribly demanding. Sometimes in our lives, everything comes at us at once. Demands are made on us, and we become terribly upset. So when life becomes difficult and complex, just take time out to do *ānāpānasati*. Try to get a perspective on things, instead of just reacting with resentment or confusion to difficult situations. I've found that I can switch over to *ānāpānasati* for just ten minutes, and it will give me a new perspective. As a result I don't get sucked into the appearance of things and get lost in confusion. I can keep perspective on the things around me, and I know how to endure and handle the conditions that arise.

So this is a way of training the mind. The breath is an object that's always present. Rather than going out there to listen to music or read a book, you are coming right here to your body. You are concentrating on something close rather than on something far away. Then, as you become more calm, you can have the *ānāpānasati* go inward to the peace and the silence of your mind. You begin to experience emptiness, or *suññatā*. You can actually hear the silence of your mind. And when you know that, you can turn to the emptiness—to the unconditioned— rather than to the breath or to the conditions of the mind.

Seeing the Way Things Are

In Buddhist meditation, we are recognizing the way things are. It's the study of nature, as we experience it. It's not the study of nature through theories in books or ideas from someone else. It's direct investigation— watching and listening. In universities, you complicate everything by learning about all sorts of things, but in meditation you simplify. You are just watching the way things are.

Doing *ānāpānasati*, you feel the breath arising and passing, and you can see that one conditions the other. But that's not all there is. There's the "knowing" of the breath; there is that which is mindful. And we apply that "knowing" to everything that goes on—to the conditioned and the unconditioned. This is a way of transcendence, of being awake, rather than trying to escape. It is all based on the ordinary postures of sitting, standing, walking, and lying down, and, most of all, on ordinary breathing.

In Buddhist meditation, you are moving toward what is most ordinary—the unconditioned. Conditions are extraordinary; they can be exciting, sometimes fantastic, phenomena. But peace of mind, the unconditioned, the silence of it, is so ordinary that no one ever notices. It's there all the time but we don't even know it because we're so fascinated by the miraculous and the extraordinary, by transitory things that stimulate and depress. We get caught up in the way things seem to be, and we forget. In meditation, we're going back to the peace that is in the position of knowing. Then, the world is understood for what it is, and we are no longer deluded by it. We can live and act in the world without being overwhelmed by the conditions we experience.

Question: In my life, I'm busy all the time. When I get home, I don't feel as if I've got enough energy to do very much. My mind's going around and around, spinning in circles. I don't think I could possibly meditate because, when I sit still, my mind's either thinking about things or I feel sleepy. How should I try to practice meditation when my mind is scrambled at the end of the day?

Answer: Well, regard meditation as recognizing the way things are. To start a meditation is always to recognize where you are right here and now, so that if your mind is scrambled at the end of the day, then just recognize scrambling. Acknowledge the feeling and the aversion to it—the wanting it to be otherwise. That is the right way of meditating. With this attitude, you'll find that your meditation will have a very beneficial effect.

If, after a hectic day, you try to stop all your mental reactions when you go home, it will lead to failure, and then you'll feel you can't meditate. So instead, you have to start using the situation as it is. You have to learn to objectify the feeling of being scrambled or the idea that you can't meditate. You have to just recognize that those feelings and ideas are objects of your mind, and that you are a witness to them. If you feel a mess and confused, then practice fully accepting that. Objectify that, rather than resisting or trying to make the confusion refined or peaceful.

Much of life is going to be a scramble; it's the way life is as a human being. We're going to get a lot of things happening all at the same time. Much of our life is going to be a lot of things coming at us at once, many of them unpleasant. Well, what do we do about that? Does it mean we can't meditate? Or does it mean we can use these difficult patches as tools for meditation rather than see them as obstacles?

If you have too many ideas about what good meditation is and how it has to be, then when those conditions aren't there, you're going to feel that you can't do it. So change your attitude from assuming that you can only meditate under the best conditions, to seeing meditation as the way you relate to life as it is—the best, the worst, or just the ordinary.

10
Cleansing the Mind

When you practice mindfulness of the breath (*ānāpāna-sati*), you learn to concentrate the mind on the breathing. If you wish, you can do it for just ten minutes at a time, as an exercise. When you're meditating for a longer time, you can do *ānāpānasati* for the first ten or fifteen minutes, until the mind becomes concentrated. If it doesn't become concentrated, just keep watching what goes wrong. You have to recognize the kind of mood you're in; you might find that it's easier to concentrate at some times of the day rather than others. Maybe you are feeling tired, or your body isn't feeling good. After a meal, concentration is very difficult because the energy of the body is taken up with the digestion of food.

After about ten minutes of intensive practice, let go, and don't concentrate on the breath anymore. Instead, watch the conditions of mind; watch what arises and passes away. Note the arising of thoughts and feelings. When you find yourself thinking, or you realize you're caught up in thought, then that moment of recognition is a point of mindfulness. But if you follow that recognition with a judgment, if you start feeling guilty or averse to having been caught up in thinking, then you are thinking again. Or if you try to figure out why you became lost in thought, you just get caught up in analyzing. So you have to keep letting go of thinking, and just observe.

At first, we don't have much continuity of mindfulness because our habit is to be obsessed with thought, to be caught up in it. Therefore, we have to practice mindfulness more or less from one moment to the next.

When we find ourselves lost in thought, we just keep coming back to the mindfulness, to seeing the thoughts and feelings arise and pass away.

Insight (P. *vipassanā*) means to see clearly, to understand that everything that arises passes away. This is the teaching the Buddha devised whereby a human being can clearly comprehend the conditions of the mind, seeing them just as conditions changing, rather than as personal qualities, or as a self. Unenlightened human beings do not see mental conditions in this way. They regard all their thoughts, memories, feelings, perceptions, concepts, and the consciousness of the body, as a self. Yet these are simply what we call conditions, and they begin and end. So in insight meditation, all we are doing is recognizing that conditions arise and pass away.

The Cleansing Process

Most people, heedless and unawakened, push things aside all the time. We repress, only consciously accepting certain things. This is a habit learned from our society: we only allow into consciousness what is socially acceptable. Having been told we should only have rational, sensible thoughts, we push aside hatred and other emotions that are nasty, insane, stupid, or dirty. But these things are still there. If we repress, we never get rid of anything; it's just that we don't look at it anymore. But it eventually comes out—sometimes in the most embarrassing moments.

In meditation, we allow things that we have repressed to come into consciousness, no matter how irrational they are. Once we allow something into consciousness and we let it go, it ceases. It is a cleansing process—like an enema. What comes out isn't very nice, but once it's out, everything feels better.

If we don't have any wisdom in life, we try to manipulate and control everyone and ourselves, filtering out what we accept, and rejecting the rest. Then when life doesn't allow us to control things, we fall apart, and everything comes pouring out—what's called a nervous breakdown. However, if you are meditating, you can have skillful nervous breakdowns. You recognize that all your unwanted thoughts and feelings are just conditions of mind, and they are not self. You can release them rather than trying to control them. So you are opening and freeing the mind.

We have to allow repressed thoughts and feelings to come up consciously, in order to cleanse the mind. However, we usually think that our consciousness is ourself, so if what is in consciousness is confused and miserable, we think, "I'm a confused and miserable person." But what we learn from meditation is that consciousness is not self; it is not a person. Consciousness is a condition in nature. When you observe the changing nature of consciousness, you know that it is not self, and this knowledge is a release mechanism for all repression. It allows the unwanted thoughts and feelings to cease.

What comes up in consciousness can be anything. It can be beautiful or ugly, good or bad, sensible or crazy. But in meditation, the quality doesn't make any difference. You are just recognizing that consciousness changes, and you see that it is not self—it is *anattā*. When you fully understand and appreciate this, you can use consciousness for release, rather than trying to select or choose what you will allow into consciousness.

With insight meditation we are not picking and choosing. We are allowing everything—even trivialities—to arise in consciousness, and we are letting them go. We are recognizing conditions purely as conditions. So it is a compassionate thing we are doing. We are not grasping at each thing as if it were a real being or a person or as "ours." Instead, we are recognizing each one as a condition. Even if we have crazy thoughts and visions, we can allow them to appear consciously rather than repress them or indulge in them. Repressing and indulging are the two extremes; the Middle Way taught by the Buddha is the recognition of conditions.

What I mean by bringing up into consciousness is that you bring out thoughts that you don't like or are frightened of. To do this, you deliberately have to think these thoughts. So you consciously think about those secrets you hope no one will ever know, those things you are most frightened of thinking. It is those repressed emotions that motivate your life, so you deliberately bring them up, in order to see them. But you must listen to the thoughts and let them go rather than believe they are anything other than conditions of mind.

Witnessing Conditions

The sensual world is a world of conditions. Its nature is unsatisfactory because it begins—and what begins ends. If something is born, it will die. So if you are looking for your true self or your eternal soul in the conditions of the world, that will only take you to despair. This isn't a doctrine to be believed; it is something to be experienced directly. The practice of meditation is intended to help us find out whether it is true or not, through observing our own sense consciousness.

You can observe whatever you are conscious of, through the eye, ear, nose, tongue, body, and mind. All the things you are conscious of are conditions—high-minded thoughts, low-minded desires, any subjective feelings you have. In meditation, we are acting as a witness to those conditions; we are being that which knows the conditions. And we recognize the limitations of conditions. We recognize that they are changing, that they are unsatisfactory, and that they are not self. You can ask yourself, "Who is it that can know?" As you meditate, you'll notice that when anger is there, you can know it. Now, if anger were your true nature, you wouldn't be able to observe it—you would *be* the anger. But anger comes and goes, is merely a changing condition; it is not you.

Now, you might understand this in theory and have had a little bit of insight, but if you really want to free yourself from the birth-and-death cycle, then you have to endure seemingly unendurable conditions of the mind. Using wisdom, you work with the conditions, investigating them so that through conscious recognition and understanding, you can allow them to cease.

The Courage to Investigate

We have to have courage in this practice to allow fears and hatred to come up into consciousness. Things we don't like—dullness, stupidity, restlessness, doubts—these are all things that we tend to push aside. We don't want to be bothered by the trivial or the foolish or the stupid; we want to point our attention toward what is important and good. We don't want to think of ourselves as having foolish thoughts.

Hatred is something we tend to repress; we don't want to be conscious of it. This is especially true because we have been told that we should only love people. We should only love our parents and never hate our children. But one can never love something on a permanent basis; love is a changing condition, and so is hatred.

In meditation, bringing hatred into consciousness is all right, because your intention is a good one. Your intention is to purify the mind, not to use hatred as a weapon against anyone. So trust in that intention. Don't be frightened of consciously hating when you are trying to free the mind from hatred, because you are not trying to send it out to anyone. In meditation, your intention is purification, and you have to have confidence in your intention. Whether you really feel that you will ever be enlightened or not, that is something else. But have confidence in your intention of inclining toward *nibbāna*.

When you are conscious of fear, it no longer frightens you. Only by heedlessly resisting it does fear gain strength in your life. When you recognize the fact that fear is only a condition, it becomes like a dragon. It looks capable of harming you, but when you actually confront it, the dragon suddenly shrivels up and is no longer threatening. It depends solely on deluding you, on making you think it's ferocious. If you say, "Oh!" and run away whenever a frightening image appears, it can have power over you throughout your life. But if you bring whatever you are afraid of into consciousness, then it can have no power. It has power only when you give it power by reacting to it.

Hence we say the mind is like a mirror: it reflects everything. But the reflections are not the mirror. The ugliest thing can come up in front of a mirror without harming it. Maybe the reflection isn't nice to see, but it's only a reflection. Soon it goes, and everything is all right. This is why we have to be able to endure the sight of nasty reflections. We have to understand that they are only reflections, and not personal problems, not personality traits. They are just conditions, like the world itself.

Reflecting External Images

It is through the senses that you experience the things that are going on around you, and this is reflected in your mind. If you go to a big city, there are all kinds of advertisements to allure you and stimulate your senses. Our societies are based on the greed principle, so we can't help having a lot of greed and lust because these are the images that are constantly being put in front of the mirror. Human creations are, for the most part, monuments to the ego; most of them aren't calming or pleasing to the senses. They can be stimulating, exciting, boring, or depressing, but very little that we create is beautiful, bringing calm or harmony.

But in the countryside, the mountains, grass, meadows, flowers, sky, streams, and waterfalls don't arouse lust; they tend to calm the mind and soothe the senses. Staying in the country after living for months in a big city is a tremendous relief, because all the senses are able to rest on what is natural rather than on egotistical human creations. So in your own life recognize what your senses are in contact with. Don't blame yourself for everything, and don't make complex personality problems over the way the world is.

The conditions in the mind can be anything, but whether they are subjective or objective doesn't make any difference—they are all impermanent, unsatisfactory, and not self. When you are frightened, that's real for you. If you meet a superman from outer space or the spirit of your dead mother, those perceptions, too, are as real as something we can all experience, like flowers or a Buddha image. But whatever it is, no matter how fantastic or coarse or mundane the condition might be, it is still only a condition in the mind.

Saying Goodbye to Unpleasant Conditions

Sometimes, as you watch the mind and allow it to open, all kinds of conditions come pouring out. During my first year in northeast Thailand, I went through some pretty heavy cleansing enemas as I began to allow things to come up in my consciousness. I would sit there, and these awful things would just be going on and on. I'd remember everything I ever did, way back into early childhood. Eventually, I had a kind of vision, almost like a schizophrenic experience. As I was sitting there, I saw my mother and everyone I knew just walking out of my brain. I thought, "This is madness, I'm going crazy." But somehow I wasn't worried about it, it didn't frighten me; in fact, I began to enjoy it. My father, my brother, my sister—everybody I knew—was walking out of my brain! "Goodbye!" The next morning I felt a tremendous release. It was like the feeling of relief when a terrible boil breaks, and the pain from it is gone. I looked around me, and everything looked so beautiful! The little hut where I was living was actually just a crude shack, but it looked like a palace. Even the toilet seemed beautiful, with the sun shining through the lattice work into a plastic dish that looked completely ethereal. I walked outside, and the little forest had a tremendous radiance. I had not seen beauty like that since I was a child.

I realized that I had learned to live in a very self-conscious way. The conditioning process, this agonizing self-consciousness of fear and desire, had become like a screen over my life. It reminded me of the dirty windows you see when people don't wash their cars, and the windows become silted up with dirt and grime so that you can't see the beautiful scenery. When I let it all go in meditation and said goodbye to it, it was like washing the windows. It was lovely to see through clean windows again. So meditation is allowing things to arise, recognizing them, and letting them go. It's a cleansing process.

Dealing with Ghosts

Now fortunately, most people don't have horrendous visions or schizophrenic subjective visions. Usually "spirits from the dead" are just whining, complaining things in the mind: "You did this to me." "You should have done that for me." Those whining little things in human consciousness seem to carry on for a while, and then they die.

In Thailand, when this kind of thing happens they say they have a ghost, so the family offers a meal to the monks. The monks sometimes go into the home and chant, "May all beings be free from suffering and sorrow." And almost every time, the ghost goes away. I don't know why—you can speculate about it—but it's always good to be generous and kind. So, if you find that you're being obsessed by some kind of spirit, do something good—give a meal to a Buddhist monk or nun, or offer help to some poor person—and say, "May this act of generosity benefit this unfortunate spirit."

People in Thailand are conditioned from the time they are born to believe in ghosts. They have fantastic ghost stories, and they talk about ghosts all the time. Even those from sophisticated backgrounds are conditioned to believe in such things; it's part of the culture. But my childhood conditioning was to not believe in those things. When I was a child, my mother and father said ghosts didn't exist. Therefore, I was able to go to the places in Thailand where there were supposed to be terrible ghosts, and I never saw any of them. When we established the Bung Wai Monastery, they gave me a place to stay in the forest where the worst ghosts lived. I didn't even know this until the third day, when somebody told me that a horrendous ghost lived there. As far as I was concerned, it was a beautiful place. Yet, people who believe in the ghost go there and actually see this ghost.

Now what is it? What does the mind do? I'm not asking you to believe or disbelieve these things, but to recognize the way the mind works. Conditions are created in your mind as a result of the way you've been trained to perceive things. If you live in a family that teaches you to believe in ghosts from childhood when you're very susceptible and open to what other people tell you, you don't question it. Even when you go to the university and have much more sophisticated perceptions, on the emotional level you still have the same fear of ghosts because of that conditioned perception from childhood. We all have fears and perceptions conditioned into us from childhood. And we have to bring them up into consciousness if we want to be free of them.

Knowing Conditions and the Unconditioned

We must recognize our fears and perceptions as conditionings, not ultimate truths. In spiritual development, we're getting to the point of balance where we recognize the conditions of the mind simply as conditions;

that is, they begin and end. Whether they are mental or physical, whether they are subject or object, they all have the same characteristics of impermanence, unsatisfactoriness, and non-self.

The unconditioned is something you can't conceive because conceptions are all conditions. It's something that has to be known directly. *Nibbāna* is the unconditioned, so when we say we are inclining toward *nibbāna*, we mean toward the unconditioned.

Now what is the unconditioned? You can't see it, smell it, taste it, touch it, hear it, or think it, yet it's where all conditions merge. It's not a sense. It is peace. It doesn't arise or pass away, begin or end. It's from there that all conditions arise. When you're bringing things up into consciousness and allowing them to cease, they cease in the unconditioned.

The goal, then, is to recognize and know conditions as conditions, and the unconditioned as the unconditioned. The goal is to be that knowing. In other words, the goal is to be mindful. It's not just a belief, it's something you have to do for yourself—no one can do it for you. And Buddhism is a vehicle, a convention to help you break through the delusions and find release from the mortal condition as you realize the unconditioned—the deathless state.

Question: How much will and effort should one put into this practice? I heard you talk about the bright and clear mind, so I thought I'd try to get my mind bright and clear and stop thinking. Trying to do that, I got really tense and uptight, but I remembered what you said about letting go, so I relaxed. But then I got all sleepy, and my mind was dribbling away. What's the nature of effort and will power in Dhamma practice?

Answer: The emphasis is on Right Effort, not on will power. In the Western world, we are often very willful. We use will power, which can be anything but Right Effort.

Sometimes, we use our minds to force and compel ourselves to do things. But then, at other times, we don't use any force and we collapse into a heap. Those are the two extremes. On the one hand, you can use too much effort for something that you can't sustain. But on the other hand, since you think of letting go as not doing anything, you use too little effort and you collapse and fall asleep.

Right Effort comes from mindfulness, in which there's always the ability to sustain. If you apply the right amount of effort for the situation, then it's sustainable. Sometimes, you have to use an enormous amount of effort in one moment, but that's only for very extreme situations. At other times in modern society, you can use very little effort and just drift along in the flow because society takes care of you—you can just get by. Right Effort is applying the amount of effort that is right for the time and place. Mindfulness tells us when it's time to just collapse and go to sleep, when it's time to use an enormous amount of effort to do something that takes tremendous energy, and when it's time to be with the ordinariness of life—just being with the way it is and not following one extreme or the other.

11

Noticing Space

In meditation, we can be alert and attentive; it's like listening, being with the moment as it is, just listening. What we are doing is bringing into awareness the way it is, noticing space and form, the unconditioned and the conditioned.

For example, as mentioned earlier, we can notice the space in a room. Most people probably wouldn't notice the space; they would notice the things in it—the people, the walls, the floor, the furniture. But in order to notice the space, what do we do? We withdraw our attention from the things, and bring our attention to the space. This does not mean getting rid of the things, or denying the things their right to be there. It merely means not concentrating on them, not going from one thing to another.

The space in a room is peaceful. The objects in the room can excite, repel, or attract, but the space has no such quality. However, even though the space does not attract our attention, we can be fully aware of it, and we become aware of it when we are no longer absorbing into the objects in the room. When we reflect on the space in the room, we feel a sense of calm because all space is the same; the space around you and the space around me is no different. It is not mine; I can't say, "This space belongs to me" or "That space belongs to you."

Space is always present. It makes it possible for us to be together, contained within a room, in a space that is limited by walls. Space is also outside the room; it contains the whole building, the whole world. So space is not bound by objects in any way; it is not bound by anything. If we wish, we can view space as limited in a room, but really, space is unlimited.

Spacious Mind

Noticing the space around people and things provides a different way of looking at them, and developing this spacious view is a way of opening oneself. When one has a spacious mind, there is room for everything. When one has a narrow mind, there is room for only a few things. Everything has to be manipulated and controlled, the rest is just to be pushed out.

Life with a narrow view is suppressed and constricted; it is a struggle. There is always tension involved in it, because it takes an enormous amount of energy to keep everything in order all the time. If you have a narrow view of life, the disorder of life has to be ordered for you, so you are always busy manipulating the mind and rejecting things or holding on to them. This is the *dukkha* of ignorance, which comes from not understanding the way it is.

The spacious mind has room for everything. It is like the space in a room, which is never harmed by what goes in and out of it. In fact, we say "the space in this room," but actually, the room is in the space, the whole building is in the space. When the building has gone, the space will still be there. The space surrounds the building, and right now we are containing space in a room. With this view we can develop a new perspective. We can see that there are walls creating the shape of the room, and there is the space. Looking at it one way, the walls limit the space in the room. But looking at it another way, we see that space is limitless.

Space is something that you tend not to notice because it doesn't grab your attention. It is not like a beautiful flower or a terrible disaster; nor is it something really beautiful or really horrible that pulls your attention right to it. You can be mesmerized in an instant by something exciting or terrible; but you can't be mezmerized by space, can you? To notice space you have to calm down; you have to contemplate it. This is because spaciousness has no extreme qualities; it is just spacious.

Flowers can be extremely beautiful, with bright reds and oranges and purples, with beautiful shapes that are dazzling to our minds. Something else, like garbage, can be ugly and disgusting. In contrast, space is not beautiful, and it is not disgusting. It's not very noticeable, and yet, without space, there would be nothing else. We wouldn't be able to see anything else.

If you filled a room with things so that it became solid, or filled it up with cement, there would be no space left in the room. Then, of course, you couldn't have beautiful flowers or anything else; it would just be a big block. It would be useless, wouldn't it? So we need both; we need to appreciate form and space. They are the perfect couple, the true marriage, the perfect harmony. By contemplating space and form we develop wisdom.

The Sound of Silence

We can apply this perspective to the mind, using the "I" consciousness to see space as an object. In the mind, we can see that there are the thoughts and emotions—the mental conditions—that arise and cease. Usually, we are dazzled, repelled, or bound by these thoughts and emotions. We go from one thing to another, reacting, controlling, manipulating, or trying to get rid of them. So we never have any perspective in our lives. We become obsessed with either repression or indulgencing in these mental conditions; we are caught in these two extremes.

With meditation, we have the opportunity to contemplate the mind. The silence of the mind is like the space in a room. It is always there, but it is subtle—it doesn't stand out. It has no extreme quality that would stimulate and grasp our attention, so we have to be attentive in order to notice it. One way to focus attention on the silence of the mind is to notice the sound of silence.

One can use the sound of silence (the primordial sound, the sound of the mind, or whatever you want to call it) very skillfully, by bringing it up and paying attention to it. It has a high pitch that is quite difficult to describe. Even if you plug your ears, put your fingers against your ears, or are under water, you can hear it. It is a background sound that is not dependent upon the ears. We know it is independent because we hear this high-pitched, vibrating sound even when the ears are blocked.

By concentrating your attention on the sound of silence for a while, you really begin to know it. You develop a mode of knowing in which you can reflect. It's not a concentrated state that you absorb into; it's not a suppressive kind of concentration. The mind is concentrated in a state of balance and openness, rather than absorbed into an object. You can use that balanced and open concentration as a way of seeing things in perspective, a way of letting things go.

Now, I really want you to investigate this mode of knowing so that you begin to see how to let go of things, rather than just have the idea that you *should* let go of things. You might come away from the Buddhist teachings with this idea, but may find that you can't do it very easily. You might think, "Oh no, I can't let go of things!" This type of judgment is another ego problem that you can create: "Only others can let go, but I can't let go. I should let go, because Venerable Sumedho said everybody should let go." That judgment is another manifestation of "I am," isn't it? And it is just a thought, a mental condition that exists temporarily within the spaciousness of the mind.

Space around Thoughts

Take that simple sentence, "I am," and begin to notice, contemplate, and reflect on the space around those two words. Rather than looking for something else, sustain attention on the space around the words. Look at thinking itself, really examine and investigate it. Now, you can't watch yourself habitually thinking, because as soon as you notice that you're thinking, the thinking stops. You might be going along worrying, "I wonder if this will happen. What if that happens. Oh, I'm thinking," and it stops.

To examine the thinking process, deliberately think something: take just one ordinary thought such as "I am a human being," and just look at it. If you look at the beginning of it, you can see that just before you say, "I," there is a kind of empty space. Then, if you think in your mind, "I—am—a—human—being," you will see space between the words. We are not looking at thought to see whether we have intelligent thoughts or stupid ones. Instead, we are deliberately thinking in order to notice the space around each thought. This way, we begin to have a perspective on the impermanent nature of thinking.

This is just one way of investigating so that we can notice the emptiness when there is no thought in the mind. Try to focus on that space; see if you can concentrate on that space before and after a thought. For how long can you do it? Think, "I am a human being," and just before you start thinking it, stay in that space just before you say it. Now that's mindfulness, isn't it? Your mind is empty, but there is also an intention to think a particular thought. Then think it, and at the end of the thought, try to stay in the space at the end. Does your mind stay empty?

Most of our suffering comes from habitual thinking. If we try to stop it out of aversion to thinking, we can't; we just go on and on and on. So the important thing is not to get rid of thought, but to understand it. And we do this by concentrating on the space in the mind, rather than on the thoughts.

Our minds tend to get caught up with thoughts of attraction or aversion to objects, but the space around those thoughts is not attractive or repulsive. The space around an attractive thought and a repulsive thought is not different, is it? Concentrating on the space between thoughts, we become less caught up in our preferences concerning the thoughts. So if you find that an obsessive thought of guilt, self-pity, or passion keeps coming up, then work with it in this way—deliberately think it, really bring it up as a conscious state, and notice the space around it.

It's like looking at the space in a room: you don't go looking for the space, do you? You are simply open to it, because it is here all the time. It is not anything you are going to find in the cupboard or in the next room, or under the floor—it is here right now. So you open to its presence; you begin to notice that it is here.

If you are still concentrated on the curtains or the windows or the people, you don't notice the space. But you don't have to get rid of all those things to notice the space. Instead, you just open to the space; you notice it. Rather than focusing your attention on one thing, you are opening the mind completely. You are not choosing a conditioned object, but rather you are aware of the space in which the conditioned objects exist.

The Position of Buddha-Knowing

With the mind, you can apply inwardly the same open attention. When your eyes are closed, you can listen to the inner voices that "speak" in the mind. They say, "I am this...I should not be like that." You can use those voices for taking you to the space between thoughts. Rather than making a big problem about the obsessions and fears that go on in your mind, you can open your attention and see those obsessions and fears as mental conditions that come and go in space. This way, even an evil thought can take you to emptiness.

This way of knowing is very skillful because it ends the mental battle in which you were trying to get rid of evil thoughts. You can give the devil his due. You now know that the devil is an impermanent thing. It arises and ceases in the mind, so you don't have to make anything out of it. Devils or angels—they are all the same. Before, you'd have an evil thought and start creating a problem: "The devil's after me. I've got to get rid of the devil!" Now, whether it's getting rid of the devil or grabbing hold of the angels, it is all *dukkha*. If you take up this cool position of Buddha-knowing—knowing the way things are—then everything becomes Dhamma. Everything becomes the truth of the way it is. You see that all mental conditions arise and cease, the good along with the bad, the skillful along with the unskillful.

This is what we mean by reflection—beginning to notice the way it is. Rather than assuming that it should be any way at all, you are simply noticing. My purpose is not to tell you how it is, but to encourage you to notice for yourself. Don't go around saying, "Venerable Sumedho said this is the way it is." I am not trying to convince you of a point of view; I'm trying to present a way for you to consider, a way of reflecting on your own experience, a way of knowing your own mind.

Question: Some people talk about *jhanas,* states of absorption, in Buddhist meditation. What are they, and how do they fit in with mindfulness, insight, and reflection?

Answer: The *jhanas* help you develop the mind. Each *jhana* is a refinement of consciousness and, as a group, they teach you to concentrate your attention on increasingly refined objects. Through mindfulness and reflection, not willfulness, you become very aware of the quality and the result of what you're doing. When you practice one *jhana* after the other, you develop the ability to sustain attention on objects that are more and more refined. You develop great skill in this practice and you experience the bliss that comes from absorbing into increasingly more refined states of consciousness.

The Buddha recommended *jhana* practice as a skillful means, but not as an end in itself. If you let it become an end in itself, you become attached to refinement and you suffer, because so much of our human existence is not refined, but quite coarse.

In contrast to *jhana* practice, the *vipassanā* meditations (insight meditations) focus on the way things are, the impermanence of conditions, and the suffering that comes from attachments. *Vipassanā* meditations teach us that the way out of suffering is not through increasing refinements in consciousness, but through non-grasping of anything at all— not even the desire for absorption in any level of consciousness.

Question: So, insight is reflecting on the grasping mind?

Answer: Yes, insight always notices the result of grasping and develops Right Understanding. For example, contemplation on the Four Noble Truths allows us to have Right Understanding, so that self-view and self-conceit are penetrated with wisdom. When there is Right Understanding, we are not practicing *jhanas* from selfish intention; they represent a skillful way to cultivate the mind, rather than an attempt at personal attainment. People get it wrong when they approach meditation with the idea of attainment and achievement. That always comes from the basic problem of ignorance and self-view, combined with desire and clinging. And it always creates suffering.

12
Now Is the Knowing

The Buddhist word for truth is "Dhamma," and it includes everything and nothing. When we're thinking in dualistic terms, we think a thing is either something or nothing, but in reflecting on Dhamma, the mind is receptive to that totality, that wholeness, in which the relationship between something and nothing takes place. If we don't know this totality, then our life tends to be entirely conditioned by our experience, and we see such conditioned experiences as reality. So we just go from one conditioned experience to another, and these experiences don't relate much to anything beyond themselves.

When we no longer see how things truly relate to one another, life becomes complicated because our mind is fragmented. We're just reacting to this and to that—to this condition and to that feeling—and we wonder why we suffer in spite of the fact that we have everything. We think that if we have everything we want we should feel happy and secure, but we are not happy because we feel a yearning for union, a longing to go back home to the One. The human heart longs to be free from the appearances of separation and isolation that we feel so strongly.

Longing for Fulfillment

The Buddhist teaching asks us to reflect on the human experience, starting with the feeling of separation and alienation that is common to all of us. If we don't contemplate our own existence or try to understand it, then our life seems to be filled with meaningless activity, and our sense of that tends to increase the feeling of separation and alienation.

We want to find someone who will fulfill us, someone on whom we can depend, someone who will never fail us. There used to be a romantic image of the person who was made for us; when we met them, we would live happily ever after in a state of bliss. But even though we might find the "right" person, it is always a disappointment if we are expecting them to fulfill us. Ultimately, they can't fulfill us because they are separate from ourselves. For example, if we attach to them and they die, we feel bereft because we are left without that on which we've depended. Anything separate from us, any other being that comes to us, will inevitably go away from us. So making a demand for fulfillment on another creature will increase our sense of alienation, disappointment, sorrow, grief, and despair.

The spiritual life, then, is one in which we no longer seek union on this sensory plane. We're no longer making demands on other beings; we're no longer expecting anything from anyone else. We're no longer even seeking God as a separate being who will come and help us, saving the day when we're in trouble. We relinquish any kind of interference or intercession from above, and we don't expect or demand that. Instead, we begin to examine the very center of being, in a way that lets us realize it within the apparent separateness of our existence.

Questioning Conventional Reality

Separation is only an appearance, but our culture believes in it as a reality. The "real world" to many people is the apparent reality of daily life: going to work, being with family, having friends—all the good things and bad things that take place within our society. We can regard these things as real, because we have to cope with them. We have to take care of our bodies, we have to make a living, we have to learn how to get along with others, we have to learn how to raise children, and we have to do everything else on this worldly, conventional plane.

I am not trying to tell you that these conventional activities are a total illusion and that they do not really exist. The conventional world is what it is, but it's not ultimately real. It is a world of changing and of shadows, a world of birth and of death; it's composed of arising and ceasing, coming and going. This is what we can label conventional reality, because it does seem very real to us. But, in contemplation, we do not simply believe in conventional reality because it accords with our own conditioning; instead we take a different position, one of inquiry.

We need to question conventional reality, not just look down on it or ignore it, but really investigate it. This is what we do in meditation. We begin to investigate that which is so ordinary to the average human being that no one even bothers to notice it. Now, we might feel inclined to question something that is exotic or extreme, but to pay attention to the ordinary seems unnecessary. So I am asking you to make a special effort to contemplate the ordinariness of life.

For example, reflect on what it's like to be in this human form, which is sensitive and feels everything, both pleasant and painful. Or ask yourself what personality is; is it really you? Don't judge whether you have a good personality or a bad one, but really question: what is personality? Investigate the realm of emotions. What is that anyway? What is the ability to feel things in your heart—love and hate, elation, depression, feeling frightened, feeling jealous, or being obsessed with desire and passion? I'm not saying you shouldn't feel hatred, or should feel only love. I'm asking you to investigate the nature of these feelings and your ability as a human being to feel them.

Contemplate the feeling of being praised. Notice what it does to your heart when somebody says that you're a beautiful or wonderful person. You can observe that feeling of happiness, rather than just being carried along in it. If somebody really hates you and criticizes you, you can be carried away with anger or resentment or grief; but, as an alternative, you can contemplate it. You can transcend the feeling realm by accepting and observing it, rather than being swept away in it or judging it.

Reflecting without Judging

We might have ideals of what a man or a woman should be. Our ideal could dictate that a man should be brave and never frightened. It might say that a woman should always be loving and kind; she should never feel jealousy or aversion to her children. When such ideals arise in our own or in other people's minds, we tend to make judgments: "Oh, I shouldn't feel like that" or "She's a terrible person, full of jealousy and anger" or "He's a coward, always protecting himself."

In our culture we are conditioned to make judgments about ourselves and each other. But the way of the Buddha is not to judge, not to suppress, not to take sides, but to notice. This is the way of the awakened mind: reflecting and noting what it is to be in this state of continuous feeling; having emotions and intelligence, being able to think and remember. Then, because we reflect in this way, we can forgive, let go, and free ourselves from the burden of these conditions and all the pain that goes with being deluded by attachments.

A human being has the ability to be alert and awake in the present moment, knowing here and now. This awakened view does not look for any particular thing because that would mean we were no longer in the knowing; we would be trying to find something to know. The awakened mind is receptive, but it's not passive and devoid of intelligence. The awakened mind is both intelligent and receptive.

Intelligence is very much a part of our human experience. We tend to misuse it because of our habit of grasping ideas and holding on to opinions. We often have quite intelligent illusions about ourselves and the world we live in. But when we let go and awaken to the moment, then there is a pure knowing, undistorted by desires and fears. The intelligence is allowed to operate fully, clearly, and brightly. This is what we're talking about when we say we take refuge in Buddha, the Awakened One. In knowing, we begin to understand how to act, and how not to act. We begin to understand what suffering really is. We learn how to not suffer, how to let suffering cease and, ultimately, that there is no suffering at all.

Accepting the Present

Suffering is the illusion that we project onto life because of our ignorance and through the habits of our unawakened heart or mind. If, instead of focusing on this illusion, we look into the present moment, whatever it is, then we can see that, "this is the way it is." By recollecting we bring the moment to consciousness. It reminds us that this is the way it is right now. We're not trying to say it should be any particular way, or that it shouldn't be any particular way. Even if it seems absolutely terrible right now, we are not judging it as terrible; we are merely acknowledging that this is the way it is.

Using the ability to reflect in this manner is very helpful in difficult personal situations, and also when we are considering the problems of the world. This is the way it is, isn't it? I'm not saying that we don't care about the way it is, but we are accepting the way it is, so that we can really understand it. We can't understand anything that we can't accept. If we want to understand something rotten, we have to accept its rottenness. It doesn't mean we *like* it; we can't like rottenness, because it's repulsive; but we can accept it. And once we have accepted the rottenness of it, then we can begin to understand it.

Try this type of reflection with your own mental states. If you judge a rotten mental state saying, "Oh, I'm a rotten person, I shouldn't think like that, I shouldn't feel like that, there is something wrong with me," then you have not accepted it. You've judged it, and either you blame somebody else, or you blame yourself. That is not acceptance; that is merely reaction and judgment.

The more you react out of ignorance—rejecting and suppressing—the more you find those very things following you about. Rejection and suppression haunt you, and you are caught in a vortex of misery that you are creating in your mind. Now, acceptance doesn't mean approval or liking, but it does imply a willingness to bear what is unpleasant, and an ability to endure its nastiness and its pain. Through endurance you find that the condition can cease; you can let it go. You can let go of things when you accept them, but until you do accept them, your life is merely a series of reactions—running away if the condition is bad, or grasping at it if it is good.

Letting Go of the Past

In our society, we are very much conditioned to believe that our memories are really ours. We don't generally remember the ordinary events of our lives, but we do remember the very good ones: we remember when we won a prize or had a wonderful romance. We also remember the bad things we have done or that have been done to us.

Grasping occurs either when we hold on and regurgitate all our memories, or when we try to get rid of them; these are the two forms of grasping. It sounds paradoxical, but we are actually clinging to something when we try to get rid of it. The more we try to get rid of something, the more we're actually clinging to it. That's why these things haunt us, because we are actually clinging to them.

For example, suppose somebody has done something terrible to you and you are angry about it, but decide not to think about it. Just try to put it out of your mind by willing yourself to not think about it. You succeed for maybe one second, and then it suddenly comes exploding back. Your desire is to get rid of it, but that very desire is the clinging process taking place. So what you have to do is not try to will yourself to push the anger out of your mind; you have to accept the anger.

You'll find a sense of peace and calm by accepting the pain that you have and letting go of it; the relief comes not by rejecting the pain, but by allowing it to be the way it is. Anything that you have to bear will eventually cease anyway, and its cessation is always a relief, because you are allowing things to flow and move according to their own nature. You are in a harmonious realm.

The past is only a memory in the present moment, isn't it? Right now, there is only now; wherever you are, it is now. Anything you can remember—what you've done, or what somebody else has done—are memories. They come and go in the mind, in the present moment. There is no past.

We believe that the past is real because we can remember it. However, I'm suggesting that you look at the past in a different way. Rather than look at it as "yours" and as "reality," look at it as it is, as something that arises and ceases in the present moment. That's what is really happening. The reality of the moment right now is that everything you remember from the past arises and ceases now. Memories don't last very long if you don't hang onto them. They just arise and cease.

Putting the Future in Perspective

What is the future? The future is what we don't remember. You can't remember the future because it hasn't happened yet. So it has to happen in the present before it becomes the past—a memory to remember. We don't know the future, but it implies infinite possibility, doesn't it? We can ignore the present by worrying about the future: "What will I do when my loved ones leave me? What will I do if I get cancer? What will I do if I lose all my money? What if I don't get enlightened before I die?"

Actually, we only die in the present; we can't die in the future because it isn't happening yet. But the future holds the possibility of loss or disease, and we know that we are getting old. These are not pleasant perceptions to most people, are they? In the future, there is always the prospect of death, sickness, and old age. There is the hope that everything will be all right—that we won't have pain, that we'll have good health till we die, that our loved ones will be with us, and that everything will be nice. However, as long as we hang onto that expectation and demand, we're also going to be pursued by the opposite.

I've noticed this from experience: as soon as I say, "I hope everything is going to be all right," immediately the opposite worry comes into my mind. If I say, "I hope we have some sunny days," immediately there is a reaction to that: I think, "Maybe it'll be one of these terrible summers where there are no warm days and no sunshine." When we attach to a hope for the future, we invite its opposite along with it.

The future is anticipation. We can be pessimistic or optimistic, but each supports the other. No matter how optimistic you are, you're still going to have to fight off the tendency toward the opposite. This is our experience of the future, until we really understand how things are, until we awaken with wisdom, clarity, and intelligence. With this new understanding, there is nothing to worry about.

Awakening to the Way It Is Now

There is no suffering; there is nothing to worry about; there is nothing to be frightened of. But if you're just grasping those words in themselves, then you are going to get their opposite. The Buddha says there is suffering, but he also says that there is the way out of suffering: "I teach two things: suffering and the way out of suffering." And his teaching is for here and now, not the next lifetime. His teaching isn't "If you're good little boys and girls during this lifetime, you'll get out of the whole thing in the next one." He is actually saying, "Right now—here and now—now is the knowing." And there isn't any suffering when there is knowing and clarity.

When we are awake to the way it is now, there is no suffering, but there is still sensitivity. There is still the coming together and the separation on this separative plane of sensory experience. There are still the ups and downs, the highs and lows of the sensory realm, and the emotion. But these are no longer seen as "me" and "mine." They are no longer grasped or rejected. Things are what they are. There is the knowing. There is the way things relate to each other, rather than the reaction to the particular condition, without an understanding of its relationship to the whole.

The more we remind ourselves of the way it is, and the more we practice, the more we feel a sense of confidence and an ability to abide in faith. Then we are able to respond in appropriate ways to the things that we are experiencing in the present. This is not a personal intelligence; it's not the intelligence you think about when you think you are intelligent. This intelligence is not conditioned by our culture, but it's receptive and learns from our life as we live it from birth to death.

With the ability to awaken and reflect on life, we free ourselves from the illusion that the body is our self. We no longer demand or expect fulfillment from that which cannot fulfill us. We no longer blame ourselves or others. All of that falls away, and there is a true and sensitive response, an understanding through being awake to the way things are. We understand the Buddha's teaching: now is the knowing.

—m—

Question: How does one make mindfulness a reality in one's life in the busy world?

Answer: Well, mindfulness is the ability to be awake and aware, wherever you are. As lay people, you don't generally have the supporting encouragement to practice mindfulness, because the people around you where you work may be not interested in Dhamma at all. However, in a monastery, you have a conventional form that encourages you. That's the advantage of monastic life.

But people need to be mindful of the way things are no matter what their lives are like, rather than making the assumption that they can't be mindful without a lot of supportive conditions. What you can't expect is tranquillity and simplicity, if you're working where there is pressure on you to be a certain way or to do particular tasks. Such pressure is not very helpful in calming your mind or in leading toward simplicity or peacefulness with external forms. But you can be mindful of it, and through that mindfulness you can find something within yourself that is peaceful in spite of the agitation and stressful conditions that surround you.

People sometimes idealize monastic life, but it's not perfect. Sometimes, you have a very nice group around you, in which everyone gets on well and is mature and sincere in what they're doing. It's very, very pleasant to be with people whom you can trust and respect, and you can get very attached to those conditions. But then somebody comes in who is disruptive, and you find yourself getting angry with them and you think, "I don't like this. We've got to get rid of this person, so we can hold on to this nice community where everyone gets on. We don't want any disruptive, unpleasant things coming into it." But that thought itself makes us miserable. So, in the monastery, we train ourselves to expand our minds to include disruptions.

You can get very attached to silence, for example, when you're on a meditation retreat. In a silent room, where everybody's still, any sound is magnified. You can feel annoyed by the rustle of a nylon jacket or somebody swallowing too loudly. You think, "Oh, I wish that person would stop making those noises." What you're doing is creating in your mind anger and aversion toward the way things are, because you want total, uninterrupted silence. But when it is disrupted, you see that you're attached to the silence. Now, including all possibilities for disruption within a situation doesn't mean you go out and try to have disrupting things happen, but you open yourself to the possibilities, rather than holding onto an idea of what you would like.

Mindfulness allows us to open the mind to all possibilities—for what we like and for what we don't like. Then we can begin to accept life's flow and movement—the way it changes—without being angry or fed up when it isn't what we want. In fact, we begin to feel quite at ease with life when we can accept the whole of it as it is. A lot of people become fussy and cowardly and timid because they don't want to get involved in anything that might agitate them or create unpleasant feelings in their minds. They think, "Oh, I can't go there because it'll just upset me." But when you're mindful, you don't mind being upset. Being upset is part of living. You don't go around seeking to be upset, but it does happen. And, when it does, you learn from it. It's part of life's experience.

13
Themes for Daily Practice

S ince many of the Buddhist scriptures are about the way of the *bhikkhu*, laypeople sometimes feel left out, as if they are at a disadvantage and there is no way for them to develop their spiritual life. Some people even think that Buddhist practice is only for Buddhist monks and nuns. So I am often asked how a layperson can practice the Dhamma. My answer is that one can practice anywhere— in the monastery or outside it, in robes or in lay life. There is always an opportunity to be with the way things are, to practice meditation, to keep the precepts as a moral foundation, to be generous, and to develop the spiritual path.

Working with the Way Things Are

It's easy to say that we should all be generous, kind, loving, and compassionate. It's easy to give advice and issue wise sayings about how everything should be. But wisdom develops in our ability to take into account the way things actually are for ourselves in our own lives; it doesn't come from beliefs about ideals. Rather, it comes from working with those things we have to bear, as well as our opportunities, or lack of them.

It's not very useful to think that we have to have the very best of everything—the best health, the best teacher, the best monastery—before we can start practicing the Dhamma. Very seldom in life do we ever find ourselves in a position where we really feel we have the best, because this is a very uncertain quality. At one moment, we might feel we have the best, and in the next, we might feel we have the worst. The perception of the best is precisely that: a perception in the mind. And if we are attached to this perception of the best, then if we have less than that, we feel the conditions aren't good enough to practice. Maybe we think we're too neurotic, we make too many terrible mistakes in our lives, we say too many horrible things. Or maybe we look around and see flaws in all the teachers we meet, or in the monasteries we go to. You can always find something wrong, something that makes it not quite fit the perfect image.

I remember people looking for the best teacher in Thailand. Wherever they went, they found something wrong. Either the teacher would be chewing betel nut and they would say, "An *arahant* certainly wouldn't be chewing betel nut." Or he'd be smoking cigarettes, and they would say, "No, we couldn't possibly learn from anyone who smokes cigarettes." It would go on and on like this. We have such high standards to judge by that we miss out on the actual opportunities as they present themselves.

So this is where our ability to reflect is most important. This is the way out of suffering. The way out of suffering is not through aiming to have the best of everything, but through being able to use wisely what we do have: the kind of character we happen to have, with all its virtues and faults, and the situation we're in, whether we are a monk, a nun, or a layperson, rich or poor, employed or unemployed.

The important thing is to reflect. Reflect on yourself, in your life. How are you living your life now? Is it terribly complicated? How could you simplify it? Are you always prone to looking for more, or to creating problems about the way you happen to be living? Really be honest and look, and ask yourself these questions. Try to use the practice of meditation to help you with your reflection.

Practicing Meditation

Sometimes, people see the practice of meditation as something that's just going to add another responsibility they have to take on in an already busy, active life. But instead of looking at it as an added task, you can take a different attitude. Attitude is something you can change. As long as you think that meditation is something you have to do, it becomes another duty added to your burden; it becomes something you should be doing, but that you don't have time for because you are so over-worked already. Now, if you just change the attitude, you can decide that meditation is as important as getting rest at night, or having some-thing to eat during the day. In fact, meditation is the most important thing in the long run, even though at times it can seem like the least important. It's important because it allows you an opportunity to have a rest from all the burdensome duties and responsibilities that you have. It allows you to let go of things, to take time out during the day to just stop and watch yourself. It helps you to observe the obsessions you might be feeling—all the energies and emotions, the restlessness, the doubts, and the worries—rather than be absorbed in them. Meditation, if done cor-rectly, helps you to stop following these mental conditions and to begin noticing them. It allows you to let them be as they are, to let go of them. When this happens, meditation becomes something you look forward to, like a good meal. It's something you really enjoy doing because it gives you a chance to break the compulsive cycles in which you can get caught up in your daily life.

Keeping the Precepts

In any kind of spiritual development, we need to establish our practice on moral principles so that we feel a sense of self-respect and stability. The five precepts (P. *pañca sīla*) provide the foundation for moral behav-ior and for lay practice of the Dhamma. They are:

- refrain from killing;
- refrain from stealing;
- refrain from adulterous or promiscuous sexual activitie;
- refrain from false speech; and
- refrain from addiction to drugs and drink.

We can contemplate these precepts and refine them. The first involves non-violence, non-killing. Most of us have not actually killed a human being. However, we've all had moments when we've felt a sudden impulse to murder somebody—at least I have. But fortunately, it's never been an obsession with me, so I've never had trouble refraining from murdering people. But violence is another thing, isn't it? We come from a society that has a lot of violence, especially violence toward lesser beings. We somehow feel it's all right to destroy the lives of other creatures.

As we develop the spiritual life, we need to live so that we are not creating violence around us, even toward the insect world or the animal kingdom. The more careful and considerate we are of other creatures, the more we can feel a sense of self-respect, the more we can feel a sense of peace and calm. Wanting to exterminate pests—wanting to get rid of some creature that's in the way or that we can't stand—is not a peaceful state of mind. So our habitual inclination is to get rid of these creatures just because we don't want them around.

Most people consider it a human right to destroy insect life. But having the attitude of non-violence (P. *ahiṁsā*) helps you to realize a sense of peace and calm; it lets you relate to other beings in a more sensitive and open way. So, refraining from using violence toward other beings (P. *pāṇātipātā*) is a precept we use as a guide for behavior in daily life.

The second precept (P. *adinnādānā*) is refraining from taking things that have not been given to us. Obviously, this applies to coarse conditions like robbing banks and cattle rustling, but this precept also suggests a more refined way of respecting the property of others. Following the second precept, you don't spend your time looking covetously at what other people have. Now, it's hard not to be covetous in a society that's constantly keeping up with the Joneses; we are encouraged in every way to look with envy at what somebody else has, and that arouses the desire to have something better. This is not a peaceful state. This is not the way to develop our spiritual life. So we take the attitude of respecting the property and the things that belong to other beings.

The third precept (P. *kāmesu micchācārā*) is refraining from sexual misconduct. People have so many miserable problems, such as guilt and fear and worry, because our society no longer understands or respects the sexual nature of the human body. We often relate to sexuality with ideas of what it should be; we don't even feel our sexuality on the natural, instinctual level. Instead, we create endless problems and self-identities about it by exalting it, hating it, fearing it, becoming obsessed with it, or feeling guilty about it. We've lost our sense of proportion about what it should be in our lives as human beings. The reflection on this precept is to understand our sexuality—which doesn't mean that you have to experience it, but rather that you begin to awaken to those very impulses, to that energy we all have. We reflect on it so as to understand it and come to terms with it in a way that we can respect. So we come to see it is not something that has to be divisive, exploitative, or selfish.

In the monastic life, we take the easy way out—celibacy. In the lay life, you take the more complicated way. Sexuality has to be considered with honesty and integrity so that we are not exploiting it just for pleasure, just as an escape, or just as an obsessive habit. If sexuality is used in ways that humiliate other people or ourselves, it can cause endless fear, disruption, and division. Adulterous behavior is always disruptive, isn't it? Even if, as in some modern marriages, each partner agrees that both can carry on in their own way, adultery is not something that will develop a spiritual life. It will not help a family to grow in respect and trust; it will only bring resentment, suspicion, jealousy, and separation. Sexuality is a vital, instinctive drive in our bodies. It needs to be understood, not judged, and it must be respected, so that it is used in a way that benefits humanity, rather than destroys it.

The fourth precept (P. *musāvādā*) is refraining from lying, gossiping, and all the heedless ways that we can use speech. It's actually quite difficult to practice this precept because our society involves us in so many negative speech habits. One way of carrying on a conversation is by gossiping, isn't it? It's socially acceptable to talk about what other people are doing, to chit-chat, exaggerate, chatter endlessly just so we can break the silence. We can also be very cruel with our speech. Although we can have high ideals—wanting to save the whales, have animal shelters, help the poor—we can still stab people with our tongues. If we are developing a spiritual life, we have to be very careful about what we say to others so that we are not intentionally causing them pain. It's inevitable that we will sometimes say things that upset people; we can't help that. But our intention should be to refrain from speaking with malicious intent. We should take on the responsibility for what we say, for how we speak, and for the suggestions we give to others.

The fifth precept (P. *surāmeraya majjapamādaṭṭhānā*) is about drinking and drugs. Now some people might think of the Middle Way as allowing us to drink moderately, without getting drunk. Others, like Theravadan monks, are not supposed to have any kind of alcoholic beverage at all, except if it happens to be in a medicine. This precept is important because, for our spiritual growth, we are developing a consciousness that isn't influenced or affected by drugs or drink.

Some people might say, "Well, I have great mystical experiences when I take LSD. I feel a Oneness with everything." Who's to deny what somebody feels under these drugs? I don't feel qualified to deny what they have actually experienced, or what they feel they have experienced. But for the spiritual life, we are not dependent upon chemicals or drugs in our system. Even if the consciousness is in the most miserable, depressed, and wretched state, even if we are feeling absolutely horrible, we are willing to start from there, rather than trying to get rid of a bad mood or a depressed feeling by taking a drug.

With our meditation, we are starting from where we are now and looking at that; we are accepting the way it is now. We don't take a drug in order to feel at one with the universe, even though we know that, with meditation, it might take a lot longer to feel that oneness. The drug is not the Middle Way, although our drug-induced impressions might be quite valid at the time. The way toward insight, unity, and oneness is not through drugs, but through Right Understanding—seeing things in the right way. Right Understanding involves seeing even our depression as something that is only a condition that we can let go of, instead of something we have to get rid of.

Affirming Our Moral Foundation

This is an extraordinary time in human history, when there seems to be license to do anything; nothing seems forbidden anymore except violent crime—and even that seems to be becoming increasingly more popular! It certainly seems to keep the daily newspapers selling! Humanity is at a point in its evolution where we don't know how to bring things together worldwide. Even though we have the United Nations, we don't trust it; we don't look to it for guidance. We don't have any overall position or institution that everyone in the world looks to with respect.

With regard to religion, we are divided into different groups—and religious groups are often famous for fighting and killing each other! People who believe in the same God are quite capable of killing each other, so even a common religious belief is not enough to bring unity.

What we need in order to have a common ground for peace on the human plane is the commitment to the five moral precepts—just that. It doesn't matter whether we believe in the same God or in different Gods, whether we believe that there isn't any God or that God is female rather than male, as long as we are committed to that which we can actually practice; i.e., these five moral precepts. That is most important for daily life.

The precepts are always stated in the negative: refrain from killing or violence; refrain from stealing; refrain from wrong sexual behavior; refrain from false speech; refrain from intoxicating drugs. When we take the precepts in Pali, we use the word "*veramaṇī*," which means "refraining from." However, Buddhist morality is not coming from an absolute or righteous position that says, "thou shalt not." Instead, the point is to refrain from intentionally taking the life of other beings. Psychologically, what does that do to you? As soon as God says, "Thou shalt not kill," it seems to stimulate us to do so. We have had a very bloody history, and a lot of the killing has been in the name of God. But taking the precept to refrain from intentionally taking the lives of other beings is a reflection. You are saying, "I will try now to be more careful, to live in a way that will not harm the lives of other beings." That is a commitment you are making. It is not God ordering you not to kill anything, but it's something that's coming from your heart, from your sense of personal integrity, compassion, and respect for the lives of other beings. So you are refraining from killing, not from fear of punishment, but from your own reflections on life, from noting that other beings want to live as much as you do.

When our Chithurst monastery first acquired Hammer Pond, there was a man nearby who taught fishing. One time I visited him, and I watched him catch fish. I was very impressed by his expertise. He was standing on the side of the stream, and I was on a little stone bridge. A large fish was on the hook, and it was struggling to get away. The fish was absolutely terrified, and it was trying desperately to get away from the hook. The fisherman was very good. He let the fish go for a while, then pulled it back up until it began to tire. He eventually pulled it up and bashed it on the head.

Later on, a fishing club came several times trying to convince me to give them permission to use the pond. They said, "We won't kill the fish. We are just going to catch them and then we'll put them back in the pond, because it's our sport. You know, we don't really want to eat them or anything; we just catch them, and then we let them go again." But noting the terror that the fish was feeling, we suddenly realize it's the same feeling we would have if we suddenly bit on a hook and somebody started pulling us out of the water. We reflect that we would react in very much the same way. Though the fish seems to the fisherman to be a stupid animal that doesn't have any feelings and doesn't really count, it is a being that is experiencing the emotion of utmost terror. That fish is absolutely terrified for his life; it's a natural reaction that all animals feel, including humans.

When you reflect in this way, you begin to see that terror isn't a personal thing. The terror the fish was feeling is exactly the same feeling we have when our life is threatened. You begin to feel a sense of respect toward the animal kingdom; you understand that animals have feelings and that they are sensitive beings. Terror is something we have all experienced in our lives already, and we can recognize it in the lives of animals when they are experiencing it. So when we reflect in this way, we don't want to cause that kind of fear in the mind of any other creature. We have no intention of doing so.

A moral foundation speaks for itself, on all religious grounds. It needs to be reaffirmed because this is the way to world peace. We need an ethical agreement, not an agreement about the reduction of nuclear weapons. That's not going to solve the problem. We still have not agreed on what is morally decent behavior for us as human beings, or as super-powers. There is no consensus as to what is morally respectable and right with regard to our lives as human beings on this planet. The moral precepts are the guide for that, whatever your beliefs. The agreement, at least, to abide by the first precept would be an enormous advancement for humanity. Just agreeing to refrain from intentionally taking the lives of other human beings would be a much finer agreement than one that reduces the number of nuclear weapons. The first, then, is the most important precept.

Being Generous

As Buddhists, we need to open our hearts. In addition to refraining from disruptive actions and speech, we try to be very generous. The virtue of generosity (P. *dāna*) is highly praised in Buddhism. In all Buddhist countries, you find tremendous generosity, for example in Thailand and Sri Lanka. Children are encouraged to offer *dāna* almost from the time they are born. You see mothers taking their little babies out to the place where monks walk by on almsround and having the baby offer some little tidbit into the monk's bowl. This starts from a very early age, so sharing what they have becomes part of their nature.

The quality of generosity impressed me very much in Thailand. If I met five little village children and gave one of them a bottle of soda, nine times out of ten, that child would divide the soda with the other children without having to be told. Now, I'd never have done that when I was that age. I'd have said, "He gave it to me; it's mine." And if my sister wanted some, I'd say, "You can't have any." But in Thailand, especially in the rice-farming areas that have kept the old values of Thai Buddhism, there is a wonderful sense of sharing that is inculcated in children from the very beginning. They get such joy in sharing a bottle of soda. Even if each child will only get one sip of it, they find it a joyful experience. They really enjoy that one sip. When you contemplate that, you see that it's much more enjoyable to have that one sip than to drink the whole bottle by yourself, not giving any to the others.

Problems arise now, with the affluence of the West and the poverty of the Third World, and the exploitative situation in which we control a lot of their economy. It's not morally right to have wonderful advantages on one side and no advantages on the other; and it's not something that we can depend on to last. Like anything that's unfair and unjust, it's going to topple and change. As people who have a sense of moral commitment, moral integrity, we want it to change. I find that I would rather live at a lower standard and share the wealth, than hoard everything and have a high standard for myself.

The sense of *dāna* is a beautiful quality of giving out; it's an open gesture of generosity, helping, making offerings. It's not a gesture of taking and getting. The gesture of *dāna* is always an open hand. It is giving away our surplus, and even giving away something that we like or need. This is a beautiful quality that helps us in our spiritual life.

Developing the Spiritual Path

Finally, there is *bhāvanā*, the development of the holy path. When there is generosity (*dāna*) and morality (*sīla*), then the spiritual practice has a foundation for development. *Bhāvanā*—the practice of mindfulness, wisely reflecting, opening ourselves to life, and learning from it—is a continuous development through this life span as a human being. It's not something you just do on a meditation retreat. *Bhāvanā* is the way we live our lives—with mindfulness, wisdom, awareness, and openness. It's looking at life very clearly as we are experiencing it and being able to adapt wisely to changing conditions.

If we are shut off in our own little world of selfishness, we find ourselves unable to adapt to change. We are threatened and frightened by anything that's different, or that goes in a way we can't trust. But with an opening of the heart and reflection on the way things are, we can adapt to anything—for better or for worse. Our guidelines are our own good-heartedness and our self-respect. They allow us to make the proper adaptations to whatever happens in our lifetime.

Often in daily life, the conditions aren't very supportive of spiritual development, so you have to learn how to use them for development.

You might tend to see them as obstacles, interfering and preventing you, and to feel aversion and discontentment with your daily life. If you think you have to have very special conditions to practice, then you will see ordinary daily life—working in the office, cleaning the house, taking care of the family—as a great imposition. Generally, these are not supporting conditions unless you change your attitude so that you can use them in your practice. You have to develop Right Understanding, the right seeing that will allow you to use daily life in a skillful way.

—m—

Question: How does monastic discipline foster spiritual development?

Answer: For monks and nuns, the monastic discipline is the vehicle that takes you to *nibbāna*. Once you get in the vehicle, you accept its limitations, and it takes you to where you're going, so you stay in it. Sometimes you don't want to stay in it—I used to feel a lot of wanting to get into some other vehicle—but you just resign yourself to it, and the result is that your life is very simple. You're not going off in all different directions. It's direct. That's why the Buddha established the monastic discipline: he realized it was an act of compassion that allows just one thing—liberation.

The problem with lay life is that one tends to go in and out of vehicles all the time. One chooses a vehicle, then gets fed up with it. One gets out of that vehicle and goes into another. So one never gets anywhere. That's the problem.

We must realize that ours is a very confused society that has little direction; yet there is great potential for the development of the human mind and heart. Western society tends to provide endless distractions, with technological toys and little perks, lures, and attractions on the sensory plane. These things distract you and keep you going from one thing to another.

But gradually, more and more people are realizing that they just don't want the distractions—they've had enough. They realize that there's something more to this experience of being human than just floating by in a convenient society.

PART III
Living the Dhamma

Irrigators channel water,
Fletchers fashion arrows,
Carpenters carve wood,
The wise train themselves.

Dhammapada, 80

14
Freedom of Heart

Freedom is a concept that many people use as an ideal for life. We want to attain some kind of freedom—physical freedom, spiritual freedom, or emotional freedom. Nobody wants to be imprisoned, bound, or tied down, so freedom becomes an ideal. It is an important concept to contemplate because we don't always understand what freedom means.

In so much of our life we are attached to ideals, and our society provides a lot of ideals for us to grasp. Freedom is one of them. But just grasping that ideal, without any wise reflection on what it really implies, takes us to discontentment, because life never seems to give us the freedom we would like to have or imagine we deserve.

Looking for Freedom Based on Desire

We can feel a continuous disappointment with life, not because anything is terribly wrong, but because life is not giving us what we want or think we deserve. We often find ourselves saying, "It's not fair." We think that things should be fair all the time. When you think about it, you see that some people are born with all the best that life has to offer, and other people are born in the most horrid and miserable states. It's unfair that there is so much inequality, isn't it? Why don't the Americans disarm? Why do Middle Easterners seem to fight all the time, bombing and ruining a beautiful city like Beirut? Why is there starvation in Africa? Why is there injustice and poverty in Central America? It's not fair, is it? It's not fair that life is like this, and our desire is for it to be different. Freedom is what we are aiming for, but we find ourselves held down by conventions and even by the physical bodies we have.

The paradox of it all is that freedom to follow one's impulses and desires doesn't seem to really bring freedom. This is how I see it from my own experience of life. I found that while I thought I was free to follow my desires, I ended up feeling very confused and enslaved by desire. There were endless choices, varieties and possibilities to feel attracted to or to be repelled by. This is our "free society." But it seems that if you just follow all these choices and possibilities, they always take you to a state of confusion.

On the other hand, in a society that has fewer opportunities in it, life isn't so complicated. For example, monastic life is not very complicated because you don't have many choices. When I wake up in the morning, I can't ask, "What am I going to wear this morning?" "How should I comb my hair?" There's not much of a choice. The monastic life looks to many people like a kind of punishment where everything is forbidden: you can't do this, and you can't do that. But what the discipline does for your mind is make life much more simple. You aren't caught up in having to make a lot of choices on the plane of sensual experience. Once you give up to the monastic life and stop resisting it and longing for more opportunities to do what you want, then of course your life has been simplified. It is much more direct and clear.

Freedom is not found in desire, but there is freedom in the Dhamma. One can make a life that is not based on preferences and attachments. And then, because one's life is not so busy with endless choices—with the many opinions, opportunities, and ideas that we are faced with in a complicated society—there is simplicity. Through this simplicity, and this moral direction, our mind (or heart) is liberated. We are able to respond and open toward life in a way that we can't when our life is complicated by desire and preference and personal attachment. Having opened to life, we can realize that freedom of the heart doesn't depend on being free to do what we want.

Now, any desire that comes out of ignorance takes us to some kind of unskillful activity or experience. With this desire, we are always going to be trying to get something, trying to get rid of something, or trying to hold onto something—because that is the nature of desire. As soon as desire gets what it wants, it starts wanting something else. I have never seen a satisfied desire, a desire that is happy when it gets what it wants. There might be some personal satisfaction for a moment when you get what you want, but then desire starts moving on to something else. So you can't be satisfied even when you get what you want, even if you have wealth, power, prestige, and the best that life has to offer. For example, if you became very rich, you'd immediately start worrying about losing all your money. There is no end to the fear of loss and the desire for gain.

As long as we are trapped in the illusions that desire creates out of ignorance, then our world is a world based on illusions. So desire never sets the heart free; it only conditions it to hope for freedom in the future. Trying to find freedom through desire only creates more bondage and more delusion.

Opening to the Dhamma

The Buddha's emphasis was on seeing through the illusions that we are attached to by examining the very nature of desire, suffering, and the cessation of desire. When we examine desire, we see that it is nothing but a movement. It is not a person, or an absolute; it arises and ceases—this is the movement of desire. If we don't let desire cease, then one desire will condition a second desire, which in turn will condition a third desire, and the process will go on and on.

The Buddhist term "mindfulness" (P. *sati*) means "to reflect, to allow things to be conscious, to bring into your mind the way things are." Now to be mindful, you have to put some effort into the moment, unless there is some immediate danger, whereupon your instinct for self-preservation makes you mindful. In normal situations, you have to exert some effort in order to observe, in an unbiased way, how things are. We learn to observe without judgment, rather than projecting something onto this moment which we then try to justify or defend. When mindfulness and wisdom work together, there is the ability to notice and to be receptive. We become sensitive to the way things are; in short, to Dhamma.

So "Dhamma" is an all-inclusive term. It means "the way things actually are, without any kind of bias." It means "the natural law." When we contemplate Dhamma, we are not coming from an idea of Dhamma as being something. If we define "Dhamma" as being this or that, then we start looking for something, don't we? So that is not the way. The way of mindfulness is the opening of the mind to the way it is—to this time and place.

Time and place are often ignored. We can be here and wish we were somewhere else. The time is now, but we are seldom really with the now of time; much of our life is spent in memories of the past, or in expectation and fear about the future. We plan for the future and we think about the past, but we don't even notice the actual here and now Dhamma—the way it is now. Then, thinking about past and future, we are caught in the power of desire, and drawn toward something else. If we reflect on our human condition in this way, it helps us to understand why the world is the way it is.

The Heart's Longing

We can see in modern life how people try to make everything fair or try to stop terrible injustices. This is a noble cause. One appreciates that. But it is not going to be enough. We end up trying to clean house and straighten it all out. Yet as soon as we make one part clean, another part starts getting dirty again. It's like trying to clean London with a toothbrush. You can't do it. You'll never find perfection in society's structures for ensuring justice, equality, and mercy because imperfection keeps creeping in.

Society will only become well ordered, fair, and just when the hearts of its people are free. As long as the hearts of the people are caught up with desires, demands, illusions, and ignorance, the best we can really do is have laws that create a certain standard. Then, if someone can't keep to the standard, they have to go to prison. That is the best we can do. We are never going to have real equality or justice or mercy in the sensory realm, because these can only come from the heart. They don't come from the eye or the ear or the nose or the tongue or the body: it's only in the heart that things are fair, and there is mercy and justice and equality.

What do we mean by the heart? This word can be used for a bodily organ, or it can be used for our emotional nature. It usually means our feelings. For example, if we are disappointed, we say we have "a broken heart." Then we have the word "mind," which refers to something less emotive. The mind deals with our intellectual process and our ability to rationalize and think; however, when we talk about our ability to feel and respond with love, we use the word "heart" rather than "mind."

All of us long for freedom in one way or another. We might hope someone else will come along and fulfill all our desires and make us happy, like Cinderella longing for Prince Charming. Maybe we are waiting for the Messiah, or for the Maitreya if we are Buddhist, or for the right prime minister or president who will set the country in the right direction. There is a longing for some external force, for something out there that we have not yet met. That kind of longing is usually fulfilled in a culture by its religion, by a spiritual aspiration toward something higher. The sensory aspects of our humanity can never really satisfy us, so we have religion to fulfill that need for human aspiration. It aims at the divine, or that which is higher, something that we have to rise up to. When you are inspired by something, your spirit goes upward rather than sinks down. When it sinks down, becoming full of anguish, despair, futility, or depression, we call that "going to hell." Your heart breaks, your spirit goes down, and you don't aspire, you don't aim at anything higher.

Birth and our sensory consciousness reinforce a sense of separateness. Sensory consciousness is a separative and discriminative consciousness that will always make us feel alienated from things. There is always a feeling of separation and conflict on the sensory plane. We can aspire to worldly things—toward wealth or fame—but that is not enough. Although we might aspire toward a worldly position, if we contemplate that, we realize a worldly position is not really what we want. We also have a natural aspiration toward rising up. This aspiration is the longing for union or non-separation. In Buddhist terms, it is the aspiration toward the Dhamma, toward truth. So with this aspiration, we rise up rather than being caught up in attachment to the senses.

Accepting Our Planetary Condition

The human body is made out of planetary elements: the solid element, the liquid element, fire, and air. We have to live on the food that grows out of the planet. We need water, we need the warmth from the sun, we need air. When our bodies die, their elements are returned to the planet; they don't float away into heaven. So in this sensory life of living within a human body, we must accept the limitations of the earthly body, rather than desire to get out of it and to turn our back on the planet. Such a desire would be a selfish delusion. We would be saying, "I don't like this planet. I'm fed up with this body. I'm going to float up into a finer, more ethereal space." Such a desire is based on the illusion of a separate self, on aversion to that separate self, and on the desire to get to something better, more refined, or more subtle. This is the movement of desire rather than aspiration.

In meditation, one of the important lessons is to accept the earth and the body. We meditate on the body a lot; in the beginning, meditation is centered on the physical body. We learn how to calm the body and how to live without ignoring the body's needs, or trying to bend it to our desires. If we don't understand our bodies, we can be quite brutal and uncaring toward them. For example, when we encounter pain in meditation, we can try to force the body to shut up and stop being painful. We can try to attain a trance-like state in which we can just forget the body. But when the body starts becoming painful or hungry, or we have to go to the toilet, then we think the body is disgusting. It's not fair, is it? We just get into one of the blissful realms and then, suddenly, we have to go to the toilet. It's not fair!

But in meditation, the aim of contemplating the body is not to take a position for or against the body, but to understand it. It is like this; bodies are like this. We are not thinking of it in a personal way. Whether it is attractive or unattractive, we simply see the body as the body. We no longer look at it as my body in contrast to your body: it is just this body. It feels like this, and it is like this, and it works like this.

When we accept it for what it is, the body does not create many problems. Bodies create a lot of problems when we don't accept them, when we dismiss them, or exalt them, or do something we shouldn't with them. Then bodies can be pretty wretched, miserable conditions we have to live with. But the body itself is not an obstacle when we accept it, understand it, and know it. This is the accepting of our planetary condition, with all that it entails: the aging process of the body, the diseases it gets, and its death. Having been born, it grows up, gets old, and dies. That's what it's supposed to do. When we see it as Dhamma, then it presents no problem. It is the way it is.

Aspiring toward the Divine

The human body isn't an end in itself. No matter how beautiful or healthy it might be, it's not what we are, so we can never be contented simply with the functions of the body. It is not what we are, so we can't ever really feel at home, or truly at ease with the body—or with the planet. There is the aspiration, the rising up toward something higher, finer, or more subtle.

When we look at planetary life, what is it like? If we study the animal life on this planet, we see that it is about survival: animals have to survive through being strong, being clever, or being in the majority. Animals can't agree on things, so they can't have laws. For example, there can be no agreement on the animal plane not to kill. Even in the human realm, we are not that much better, are we? We are very destructive creatures, quite willing to kill each other, and kill the animals, but we can aspire to be higher than that. If we were only animals, then we wouldn't even be able to think of something better. There would just be the law of the jungle, and the survival of the fittest; we wouldn't even have a concept for anything higher than that. But we do. We can think of justice and equality and of being fair; we have a mind that can conceive of such possibilities. And that is an aspiration of the human spirit toward a higher plane than that of mere survival.

The mind that sinks down says human beings are just animals anyway: survival of the fittest is a law of nature, so that is just the way it is. This mind thinks we are no better than other animals, and we just have to accept it. We should each get what we can for ourselves because we've got to survive. This mind thinks, "I've got mine. If you're too stupid and weak to get yours, tough luck; that's it, too bad." This is a pessimistic, fatalistic sinking of the spirit to a lower level. But speaking from my mind, I know that I aspire to something higher than that, and I can see that people around me do as well. Human beings can aspire toward the divine.

Now, when we think of the divine, what does that really mean? "Divinity" is not usually a word we use in Buddhism. Often, people come to Buddhism because they are fed up with divinity. All that talk about God and the afterlife—they are fed up with it. They don't believe it. They want something more realistic. They are not aiming for something after death, or in the next life, something they can't see, or know, or touch. But if there were nothing divine, then we wouldn't be able to conceive of divinity. Our ability to conceive of it comes from having touched upon it in things that we actually know and experience—at least in momentary flashes.

Divinity in Kindness, Compassion, Joy, and Serenity

The kindness of a mother to a child is a kind of divinity, isn't it? That's an experience of divinity. Selfless giving, just because somebody needs something—sacrificing personal privileges and conveniences for the welfare of others—that to me is a touch of divinity. When we are really fair and honest with things, when we are not coming from a prejudice or a bias, when there is joyfulness and serenity of mind, when the mind is clear and not bound into inferior states, we are in contact with divinity.

Rather than talk about divinity, Buddhists say, "Our intention is to realize *nibbāna*." What does *nibbāna* really mean? This refers to the realization we have when we are not grasping anything. In that realization, we experience the selfless qualities of kindness, compassion, joy, and serenity. We make a connection with something higher; we are in alignment with the divine; and we experience true ease, peacefulness, and bliss.

If you were going to meet a divine being, what would you expect that being to be like? What perception comes to your mind? For example, when you think of Jesus Christ, probably the perception of compassion comes along with that thought. Well, if there is divinity, then compassion is a divine quality. When I look at what happens in my own mind, I notice that when there is no self-interest or demand in life, the feeling that arises is compassion. This is not something that I project onto a situation; it happens naturally. When there is no personal desire for gain or anything else, then compassion manifests for the unhappiness and confusion of other beings. This compassion isn't a sentiment, coming from an idea of how it should be; it's not like that. It's an understanding of the way things are, and how much suffering there is in the world because of ignorance.

In contrast, feeling sorry for people can arise from personal fear. Somebody has cancer, and we think, "Oh, that poor person has cancer; I'm glad I don't have it. I hope I don't get it." Then we project our own ideas onto that person. But that is not compassion. Compassion is being truly open to the suffering of others, not because we personally want anything from them, but because there is willingness to be patient and to be with the miseries that other people are enduring. We are willing to bear with the misfortune, sadness, and misery that we see around us, without trying to get out of it or blame anybody for it. That is compassion; that is what I would call a divine quality.

Joy to me is the feeling you have when you see that what is truly beautiful in life is to associate with the good. It is a very positive feeling, and it does not come from wanting to possess the good or the beautiful—there is no joy in that. Joy is a spontaneous way to relate to the beautiful, the good, and the true in other beings and in everything. In this joyfulness, there is none of the envy and jealousy that come when the personal side gets involved. If we are still caught in a self-view, when we see somebody truly beautiful and good, we can be envious. We think, "He is better than I am." And we might go on to say, "He might be good, but..." We put them down, don't we? If we can't delight in beauty, truth, or goodness unless we can own it, then that is not joy. That is greed. The true experience of joy is another divine quality.

Serenity of mind comes when the mind is calm and cool. The serene mind is able to be with life, with the way things are, without being attached. Then the mind is even, knowing, and bright. So that is another experience of divinity.

Freedom is *nibbāna*, the realization of that non-grasping state in which we experience true kindness, compassion, joyfulness, and serenity. We may talk about freedom in relation to being fair and just, but what I am talking about is the aspiration of the human heart toward the divine, toward oneness and non-separation.

So what is freedom of heart? Well I would say it is our freedom of choice to either rise up or sink down. Which one do you want to choose? In any given moment of our life, we can feel sorry for ourselves, thinking about all the things we don't like and all that's wrong with the world, or we can choose to reflect on the Dhamma, try to understand it, and follow our aspiration toward the divine.

—⟁—

Question: When I think of freedom, I think of spontaneity. If all the time when you're being mindful you're observing and watching everything before you do anything, doesn't that mean you lose spontaneity?

Answer: No, but you've pointed out a difficulty with language. When one says "watching and observing," it sounds as if there's somebody who's busy doing something. However, mindfulness doesn't mean that you become somebody who's so busily observing everything that you can't respond to situations. Spontaneity has to come from faith, doesn't it? You can't hold onto an idea about how things should be and try to be spontaneous.

To be spontaneous you have to trust and, in Buddhist terms, the foundation of trust is in Buddha-Dhamma-Sangha. When that trust becomes a strong foundation, there's no need to mistrust or be anxious about life's experiences. Spontaneity operates from that trust, which is not based on personal view. Bare attention—mindfulness—allows us to respond to life's experiences spontaneously, because we put our faith in Buddha-Dhamma-Sangha. We are more spontaneous, because we're not coming from the basic delusion of a self that has to protect itself. The whole delusion of "I'm somebody who has to be on my guard against evil forces, otherwise I'll be overwhelmed" falls away. There is recognition, knowledge, and purity of heart in which one trusts and abides. The rest takes care of itself.

15

The Science of Goodness

When I was a layperson, it became apparent to me that I was not living in a way that I respected; I was living a rather foolish and not very skillful life. I could also see that, because I did not respect the way I was living, I was unable to respect myself. Once I became a monk, things began to change. Because of my determination to live within the boundaries of the monastic form, a sense of self-respect gradually developed. I began to respect myself because I respected what I was doing, the way I was living, my intentions, my efforts, and what I had put into my life. Now, I'm not saying that everyone should become a monk or a nun, but I am saying that we should encourage self-respect in ourselves by trying to be good.

Many people can be quite diligent about meditation, but they neglect the moral precepts. Such precepts should be the foundation for all human relationships. As human beings, we need to rise up to a standard of morality and virtue. When we don't respect ourselves, we sink down into doing things the easy way, into just getting by, into ways that cause division, suspicion, and mistrust. Society now is suffering with terrible problems: drug addiction and alcoholism, corruption and murder. All these things are quite common now because people are not willing to keep a level of moral integrity. And if we don't maintain this level, we begin to sink down into depression, despair, and self-hatred.

Rising Up to Virtue

As human beings, we are not restricted to the instinctual behavior of animals; we have the ability to rise up to virtue. So our life can be devoted to developing virtue, not only through meditation, but also by living responsibly within our society. Living a life of virtue brings joy, peace, and harmony to ourselves and also to society.

I like to think of virtue as the science of goodness. We study goodness; we are not just holding opinions about it, and talking about it in some abstract way. We are actually contemplating what goodness is. We ask, "What is there to do in our lives that is good?" We make our lives a study in the science of goodness.

Many people mistake Buddhism for a fatalistic and passive religion in which you don't bother to do anything but sit and watch your breath or your navel, or sit under a tree and say "everything is impermanent." But Buddhism is not meant to be a religion of passive indifference, uncaring about the society we live in; it definitely encourages us to develop virtue, and that gives us joy in our lives.

Without joy, the religious life is impossible. And to be truly joyful, you have to be unselfish and giving; you must do things for others. This joyfulness comes from unselfish giving, in which there is no demand for any reward or recognition. If you are giving in order to get something in return, you will not find joy in your giving; you'll always feel a bit disappointed. It will never feel quite right if you want something back in return. So the joy of giving, of loving, of being able to do good things, of helping others, is beyond selfishness. It is its own reward. It's an honor to be able to do things for other people, to live in a way that is for the welfare of the society, rather than taking advantage of society.

Living Responsibly on Our Planet

We are living at a time when we need to look more deeply at ourselves and the world that we share with all other beings. We can no longer think in terms of isolation, or of living for ourselves alone. In the past fifty years it has become obvious that all of us on this planet are related to each other, just by the fact that we are all planetary beings. So when one group has privileges and another doesn't, there is an imbalance, and this will always create some kind of conflict. Wherever there is injustice, unfairness, or imbalance, the result will be an increase in suffering in the human realm, as well as in the lives of all other creatures. So it is wise now to reflect on the fact that we are all interrelated, and that we are all supporting each other. We are not individuals or nations that can operate independently, disregarding the effect we have on the rest of the world.

Nowadays, many more people are beginning to ask, "What should I do with my life? Can I just live it according to my impulses and the fashions of the time, doing just what I feel like doing or not doing? Do I really have the right to live life just for my own safety, security, satisfaction, and pleasure?" Since each being is a part of the whole, we have to consider what our responsibility is with regard to the society we're living in, and to the planet we share with others.

If someone is a selfish, small-minded being, they may think, "I'll get what I can for myself, even if it's at the expense of everyone else." They scheme, manipulate, and control circumstances for their own benefit, at the expense of everyone else. That's what people do when they don't have a sense of personal responsibility in their lives. In our modern age, personal responsibility has been a rather unpleasant issue for some people. It's been an issue to be avoided.

Now in fact, modern politics often plays upon this selfish interest in the citizens of Western democracies by promising all kinds of advantages, opportunities, and securities. That appeals to us in one way, because sometimes we don't feel that we are really strong enough or capable enough to be responsible. We feel that we still need a protector of some sort, some kind of parent who will take care of us, pat us on the back, tell us everything is all right, and provide for all our needs. That's tempting; there is the child in all of us that sometimes cries out for some external force to guide, nurture, and comfort us when we feel insecure.

Modern governments are often pressured into fulfilling that role in some way or another. One notices in Western democracies how demanding the citizens can be, making unending claims on the government for rights, privileges, and all kinds of opportunities. I've noticed in Britain and America that there is very little gratitude for the good things our governments have provided. We tend to dwell in a state of worry about things that might be taken away from us, or think about the things we don't like and don't want.

Then, sometimes we feel the government has failed us—just the way people sometimes feel God has failed them, or their parents haven't loved them enough. In spite of all the generosity, security, and benefits we might have received from our parents, from the government, or from God, we still find ourselves suffering; we still find ourselves discontented. It's not enough. There is not enough in the universe to truly satisfy, to give us complete satisfaction and complete contentment. There is no possible government that we can conceive of, or create, that will be able to truly satisfy all our desires for security.

In the West, our attachments have become complicated. Not only do we demand physical security, shelter, food, clothing, and medical care, but we also demand all kinds of other opportunities. We demand education, freedom to do what we want, time to live our lives in our own way, and also the opportunity to develop our individual talents and abilities. We expect so much. And yet, how much have we offered? What can we offer back? Is there perhaps something each one of us should do in order to give back? What is it that we need to know in order to stop acting like a perennial child, endlessly demanding nourishment and safety from Mother?

Not Taking Sides

At this time, there are many pressures on people to take sides in various ways. Our minds easily look for a fixed position to hold on to. The position can be a political view, a religious view, a national view, or a personal view. It can be a view about class, race, or sex. People desperately take sides on the most ridiculous issues. We feel the need to adopt some particular position that we can use to feel a sense of purpose and meaning in life. If we didn't have an opinion, we'd probably be considered a hopeless bore.

Yet we begin to see that when we do take sides—when we attach to a particular viewpoint—we tend to become obsessed with that side, and we can lose our perspective. We can be so caught up in our righteous views and behavior that we lose all sensitivity, even toward our own group or family, not to mention the opposite side. We can be so fanatically dedicated toward a political viewpoint that we are willing to destroy the whole world just to hold to this view.

Of course, only the extreme type of human beings would fall into that trap. Most of us do have some sense of perspective, but we tend to wobble and waver. We become confused because we are not quite sure on which side we should align ourselves—whether we are fully left or fully right—so we wobble between the two. Sometimes we can even feel envy for those who are very sure that their side is absolutely right at all times, and we wish we could be that strong, that convinced. We imagine how secure we'd feel if things were as clear-cut as that.

But most of our life is in this realm of neither right nor left. We are just getting on with life as best we can on the physical plane, trying to get along with the people around us, trying to find some peace and friendship. Even the most dire fanatics have to come to terms with the facts of life. They have to eat food, find a place to live, and clothe the body; they get old, suffer from illnesses, and lose loved ones. We all suffer from the desire of wanting things we don't have. And there is the inevitable death that we all must experience.

The teaching of the Buddha relates to life as it actually is. It allows all of us to open our minds to life, without being forced to take a position. This is not to say you shouldn't have any viewpoints, any opinions whatsoever; we need to have opinions in order to live in the world. But we also need to reflect on the tendency we have toward being attached to opinions. This tendency is a particularly strong problem with Western civilization: we have become very idealistic and completely caught up in theories and views about how everything should be.

Nowadays, people have very high standards; they know how everything should be. I meet very few people who are deliberately mean, uncaring, and selfish; those are rare. Most of the people I've met would like to have everything at its best—whatever "best" might mean to that particular person. We can conceive with our minds how things *should* be, and that's why we become so critical. We can see that society isn't really what it should be: it should be better. We can become so aware of the things that have gone wrong—the inefficiency, the bureaucracy, the injustices. These become dominant in the mind because we can imagine a utopian society in which everything is as it should be. We can envision the paradise where everything is fair, equal, kind, and loving. But what we experience is life as it is. How is it for you? What is your life really like?

This is what we call opening the mind to the way it is, not criticizing or affirming anything, but being truly sensitive to the good and the bad, to justice and injustice, the day and the night, the sun and the rain, the heat and the cold. In Buddhist terms, this is being mindful. The way out of suffering is through mindfulness. When it is fully present without judgment, the mind is full, open, attentive, and receptive.

With mindfulness, we are not forced to take positions, take sides, get caught up in the quarrels and problems of our families, organizations, and societies. Rather, we are able to open the mind to each conflict. The mind is capable of embracing both sides; it can be sensitive to everything. It can be open, receptive, and clear with regard to the right and the left, the good and the bad.

Taking Personal Responsibility

With mindfulness, we can be independent of the positions other people are taking. We can stand on our own two feet and take responsibility for acting in a virtuous way, regardless of what the rest of society is doing.

I can be kind, generous, and loving toward you, and that is a joy to me. But if I make my happiness dependent upon your being kind to me, then it will always be threatened, because if you aren't doing what I like—behaving the way I want you to—then I'm going to be unhappy. So then, my happiness is always under threat because the world might not behave as I want it to.

It's clear that I would spend the rest of my life being terribly disappointed if I expected everything to change—if I expected everybody to become virtuous, wars to stop, money not to be wasted, governments to be compassionate, sharing, and giving—everything to be just exactly the way I want it! Actually, I don't expect to see very much of that in my lifetime, but there is no point in being miserable about it; happiness based on what I want is not all that important.

Joy isn't dependent on getting things, or on the world going the way you want, or on people behaving the way they should, or on their giving you all the things you like and want. Joyfulness isn't dependent upon anything but your own willingness to be generous, kind, and loving. It's that mature experience of giving, sharing, and developing the science of goodness. Virtuousness is the joy we can experience in this human realm. So, although what society is doing or what everyone else is doing is beyond my control—I can't go around making everything how I want it—still, I can be kind, generous, and patient, and do good, and develop virtue. That I can do, and that's worth doing, and not something anyone can stop me from doing. However rotten or corrupted society is doesn't make any difference to our ability to be virtuous and to do good.

Benefitting Society

Now we could make society better if, rather than exploiting it, making endless demands on it, criticizing it, and disparaging it, we tried to live in a way that would help it and encourage it to do the right things. This would not only bring joy into our lives, but would also be of benefit to the society we live in. Our offering to society can be our willingness to try to live in a way that does not create fear in our own minds or in the minds of those around us.

We can move toward this attitude in our daily lives by living in a way that lets us respect ourselves. When we do that, we find that other people also respect us. And when other people respect us, then they listen to us, they pay attention, they emulate, and they follow our example. So in that way, more and more people begin to feel the joy and the freedom of being responsible for their lives.

Individual responsibility is the foundation of any society because a society is a group of individual human beings. Morality, if it's to be true and skillful, has to come from the wisdom of individual human beings. If you try to impose morality on people, then it becomes a law that can be very oppressive. The word "morality" is a bit threatening to us because we know that it can become tyranny if it is imposed on us.

But when we fully understand it, morality brings a sense of joy and self-respect and, because we begin to feel respect for ourselves, we feel respect for the right of other beings to exist. This is very peaceful. It's a lovely feeling to have self-respect and to care about the lives of others. But it has to come from wisdom and growth within. It has to come from personal responsibility and personal knowledge of oneself.

I'm not talking about superficial niceness and goodness—a mask, a pretty facade of goodness—but rather a profound goodness, in the heart of things. Virtue is something very deep and profound and penetrating. It takes wisdom, sensitivity, receptivity, and intelligence to be truly virtuous.

Question: Morality is obviously a good foundation for an individual, but it doesn't really seem to help much as a defense against evil. We seem powerless to do anything about the evil forces in the world.

Answer: That's because resisting evil out of aversion and prejudice tends to create more conflict. But that doesn't mean we should resign ourselves to the presence of evil forces and let them run over everything. We need to commit ourselves to a moral foundation. This is greatly needed in solving global problems because nowadays, morality is not a necessary condition for the operation of our nations, so there's no ground for trust. How can two governments trust each other if they both are representing immoral and untrustworthy nations that tell lies about each other or are constantly trying to frighten one another? How can you talk about world peace with this tremendous lack of commitment to moral principles?

If scientific technology had a moral basis, it wouldn't have made nuclear weapons: weapons are for killing and for creating fear. If we really want world peace, then we should have moral agreements, rather than nuclear agreements. Then we would be asking humanity to rise up to moral values, rather than just keeping people in line through fear.

If education were aimed more at ethics—getting children to look into actions, speech, and their results—then the problems of society would diminish considerably. But I don't think they teach very much of that in the schools, because it's not considered an important thing to learn. The sense of moral responsibility has definitely diminished, which is frightening, and it's not being encouraged within our youth.

Yet, in fact, children respond to that teaching beautifully. Their minds are such that you can put anything into them. But that's also a problem; because they're innocent, you can put rubbish into their minds, or you can put in really beautiful things. My choice would be to put the beautiful things in, things that arouse self-respect, kindness, and virtuous living, rather than rubbish and fear and conceited views.

For our young people, we need to stress cooperation, rather than competition. A cooperative system allows a complementary relationship, in which you're not saying, "This is the best way to be, and if you can't do it, you're inferior." A cooperative system allows for all the different types of people to work together: the fast, the slow, the young, the old, the clever, the not so clever, and so forth. There's room for everyone.

Question: Sometimes I'm paralyzed because I keep thinking and thinking about what to do, looking at it from every angle, but I don't act. How can I practice the science of goodness in this situation?

Answer: When we think too much, we can go crazy; we can get depressed or pulled into a vortex of thoughts that drag us downward. If you think too much, you can't really do anything. You have to stop thinking about it to do it. We can think, "Should I do the dishes, or shouldn't I do the dishes? Do I feel like doing them? Is doing the dishes really me? Should men do the dishes and not women, or women do the dishes and not men, or should both do them together?" And all the while, we're just sitting there.

But if you look at the task in a different way, you can approach it more positively. You can say, "What an honor to be able to do the dishes!

They are honoring me by asking me to do the dishes." Putting your hands in soapy water with bone china is a pleasant physical sensation, isn't it? If you start looking at the positive side, then you're not going into depression about washing the dishes. And you're not spending a lifetime on the same old boring reaction against washing the dishes, perhaps because your mother made you do them when you were a child.

Little issues like this hang on from our past. You can see it with men sometimes, the way they react to women: "No woman is ever going to tell me what to do. No woman can boss me around." These are the kinds of male reactions that you develop when you are rebelling against your mother. And then women can have the same attitude toward men, rebelling against their fathers: "It's male chauvinism. They're trying to dominate and pull us down. They're tyrannizing women." Sometimes we never outgrow our rebellion. Sometimes we carry that on through a whole lifetime without really knowing we are doing it.

In our reflections on Dhamma, we begin to free the mind from these very inadequate and immature reactions to life. We find, in this rising up to life, a sense of maturity and willingness to participate in it. We tend to respect people who are in positions of authority rather than rebelling or resisting out of immature habits. When we are mature, when we understand Dhamma, we can work in the world in ways that are of benefit, in ways that harmonize, in ways that are of use to the society we live in.

Question: Sometimes it's not very popular to do what is good. How can we find the courage to live a moral life?

Answer: It has become apparent to me that it is better to die than to do something evil, because we are all going to die anyway. Death is going to meet every one of us, so it doesn't really make that much difference when it happens. But evil actions are going to haunt us all our remaining life, even if we live to be one hundred years old. If we commit heedless and selfish actions, that memory will haunt us through the rest of our life, making our life miserable.

When it became apparent to me that it was better to die than to do evil, I could see that death is nothing to fear. It's the natural process, something all of us will experience, anyway. But evil action is what is truly dangerous to us; this is what we should be most wary of.

Once we realize that the most important thing is the moral quality of our speech or action, it becomes easier to find the courage to do what is good.

16

The Human Family

At this time in human history, the whole structure and foundation of our society seems to be breaking up. One used to feel that there was stability in family life and that it provided a foundation for society. But now, even the nature and purpose of the family seems to be under attack, and people don't know what to do. Our society is questioning, "What is the purpose of family life? Is it worth reviving? Is it something we should try to improve and develop, or is it something from an ancient time that we don't need anymore? What are its advantages and disadvantages?" These are all questions for our reflection and consideration.

I don't want to tell you what you should do as a family or what a family should be, as if it were an ideal to which everyone should try to conform. That would be arrogant. As a Buddhist monk, although I don't have the pressures of conventional family life, I am in the position of teaching meditation, so people confide in me and express how they are feeling. This has given me a particular perspective on the problems and experiences families tell me about. Therefore, I'd like to relate my own reflections on family issues.

The Individual and the Family

At present, we tend to be more concerned with ourselves than with our families. This is an age in which individualism has been emphasized to the point of absurdity. The opportunity that we have to develop as individuals in the modern world is quite amazing, isn't it? Each of us has been given free rein to be a self-sufficient, independent person. We are told to be personalities, to develop our creativity, to develop our lives in any way we want as free individuals. We can do what we personally want to do, whether our family likes it or not.

Now, the problem with glorifying individualism as an end in itself is that it promotes a neurotic and meaningless existence. Just being a free agent—an individual who can do what he or she wants—can give us certain pleasant moments, and we can appreciate that in some ways. But at other times, it is very depressing not to be truly related to anyone, not to be able to serve anyone. There is something in all of us, both men and women, that makes us want to give of ourselves. We would all like to sacrifice or give ourselves to another person or to a cause, to something that is beyond ourselves.

Living the religious life is a giving of oneself—to the Dhamma, to God, or to whatever is the ultimate truth in a particular religion. The purpose of monasticism is to give of yourself completely. You let go of the desire for personal reward or acknowledgment of any sort, just to be able to become a good monk or nun, and to give yourself totally to the refuges of Buddha, Dhamma, and Sangha.

The ideal of family life is for a man and woman to join together to give themselves to each other. So the sense of being one independent person has to be sacrificed for being a couple. Then with the ensuing children, the couple becomes a family, and has to give up everything for the children.

I see how parents must surrender totally to the needs of their children, and I find it very admirable. It seems to be about twenty-four hours a day of continuous giving to another being. In some ways it must be exasperating and annoying, but in other ways, it must be very fulfilling. You can see that parents can really give wisely, not out of necessity, but out of real reflection and understanding of the situation. They get tremendous joy out of giving up personal interest, privacy, rights, and much more for a helpless child.

These days, there's a lot of confusion about the roles of men and women because the traditional roles are now in question. We can no longer take for granted that "a man's duties are these" and "a woman's duties are those." In my mother's generation, they could take them for granted because the roles were more clearly defined. Even now the roles are unquestioned in more traditional societies, such as the rice-farming communities of northeast Thailand. Everybody knows what they are supposed to do. The social structure, the whole way of life, is accepted as natural, as being in harmony with nature, so no one questions it.

But then, especially when you are educated, you start questioning when you leave the security of a situation. You start reading, and you start listening to other people. You hear different views and opinions, and you begin to doubt. You ask, "Does life have to be just like this, or is there some other way of looking at it? Does a woman have to be just this way? And if she changes, is she wrong or right? What should a man be? What is the duty of a mother and of a father?"

Traditional Roles

I'd like to summarize the advice in the Pali Canon on the duties that people have in their various roles. These are the guidelines of an Asian culture from 2,500 years ago. The *Sigālaka Sutta* lists the duties of virtually all existing human relationships, including parents and children, pupils and teachers, husbands and wives, friends, masters and servants, and spiritual teachers and their disciples.

The first guidelines are about parents and children. Parents should not let their child do evil, but should encourage the child to do good. They should see to it that he or she receives training in the arts and sciences, find a suitable spouse for him or her, and give over their wealth at the right time. Children, in turn, should help look after their parents' affairs, ensure the endurance of the family name, conduct themselves in ways that make them worthy to receive inherited wealth, and make offerings in the parents' memory when they've died.

I don't remember ever getting advice like that. In fact, my parents said, "We want you to grow up and be completely independent of us. And for our part, we hope to save enough money so that, when we are old, we will never have to be dependent upon you." There was a sense of independence on both sides. Clearly, we have a different model for how parents and children should behave toward each other in our modern society.

The second set of guidelines is in reference to pupils and teachers. A pupil should stand up to receive the teacher as a sign of respect, wait attendance on the teacher, pay attention to what the teacher says, and learn with a respectful attitude. The teacher, having been upheld in these ways, should lead a pupil well, keep nothing about the subject matter secret or undisclosed, praise the pupil among friends, and protect and look after the pupil. Unfortunately, nowadays, very few pupils receive such nurturing from a teacher, and most teachers would be surprised to receive such treatment from a pupil.

The third set of guidelines is about husbands and wives. A husband should praise his wife, affirming that she is truly his wife; he should not look down on her; he should not be unfaithful; he should let her be in charge of the home, family, and money; and he should give her trinkets and adornments. A wife, in her turn, should organize the family affairs well, help the husband's relatives and friends, not be unfaithful, look after the family property, and be energetic in her duties. This is the advice for a traditional marriage; it presents an ideal of what each partner is expected to do. These are the guidelines for a cooperative relationship, in which there is mutual support and respect, rather than independence, individual rights, and conflicts.

The fourth set of guidelines concerns the relationship between two friends. One should share things with a friend, talk pleasantly, do things that are useful, be even-minded without pride, and speak truthfully without pretention. In return, the friend should give protection and protect one's property when one has been careless, give shelter when there is danger, not abandon one in a time of adversity, and uphold one along with one's relatives.

The fifth set of guidelines is regarding masters and servants. A master should arrange their servants' work so that it is suitable and in accordance with that their strength, give them food and rewards, look after them and nurse them when they are sick, share unusual or tasty delicacies with them, and give them time off. A servant should get up in the morning and start work before the master, finish work after the master, take away only that which is given by the master (in other words, not steal from him), constantly try to do better work, and praise the virtues of the master.

The final set of guidelines is about the relationship between spiritual teachers and their disciples. A spiritual teacher should encourage a disciple to do good, help them with a compassionate mind, tell them things they had not previously heard, make clear things they had already heard, and tell them how to attain the heavenly realms. A disciple should support the teacher through loving-kindness, with actions of body, actions of speech, and actions of mind. In addition, the disciple should welcome the teacher into his or her house, and the disciple should provide the requisites of food, shelter, clothing, and medicine.

These guidelines represent the traditional Buddhist advice regarding relationships. But right now, in our culture, we have to contemplate for ourselves: "What is a relationship? How should we relate? What do we expect? What do we want or demand? And what are we willing to give?" We have to ask ourselves these questions, and consider whether we know how to relate to another person.

Finding Balance without Traditional Roles

If we come from the idealistic position that believes "we are all equal, we are all exactly the same, there is no difference," then in many situations our relationships will be very difficult to define, won't they? Who's going to do the dishes? Who's going to empty the dustbin? Who is going to lead? Who is going to follow? If we all feel we are the same, then we can become confused because we don't know how to relate to each other in a structure or in a hierarchy of duties and responsibilities. So sometimes, if we are attached to the ultimate view of equality and freedom, we can become very confused, disgruntled, and even threatened by the practical side of life.

In the practice of Dhamma, we are opening the mind to the way things actually are. We begin to notice that nature itself is hierarchical, that there is always form or structure, and that when you have form, you are always going to have sequence. One is always going to be followed by two, and two is always going to be followed by three; A is followed by B, and B is followed by C. You can't say A is the same as B. If you spelled everything with an A, it would be meaningless, wouldn't it? In the conditioned world, we recognize that there are sequences.

Now if we take a fixed position on hierarchy, we become tyrannical. Someone who says they have to be the boss at all times—always number one and never number two—becomes a tyrant. But, on the other hand, an idealistic egalitarian, someone who says we must always be equal and always the same, is setting up the situation for confusion and contention. When it's time for a meal, everyone wants to be first in line. But if we are willing to designate a sequence, we can relate to that sequence. That's a relationship. You are relating as senior or junior, teacher or student, parent or child. A sequence provides a structure for relationships, so that we know how to live with each other without endless conflicts and confusion.

In the monastic life we have a particular form and structure to which we all agree. It's a voluntary life. It would be a tyranny if everyone were forced to become monks and nuns and live within the structure. But because people join the community by choice, it is not a tyranny; it's a cooperative, harmonious way of living.

You can apply these principles to family life. If you, as mother and father or husband and wife, do not decide on some clear guidelines for duties and responsibilities, then who is going to do what? Who is going to go to work? Who is going to stay home? Who is going to do the dishes? Who is going to take care of the children when they are ill? What are our duties and responsibilities in relating to each other in a family?

In America, there is very little supporting structure of this sort, and there is a total rejection of hierarchy. The American view is always the very idealistic one that we are all equal. But in England, there is much more respect for hierarchical positions. It's part of the culture with a queen, a royal family, and a class system. Even though there are many disadvantages to such a system, it also has some advantages. It gives you a clearer understanding of how to relate in different situations.

When I lived in north Borneo for two years, I had servants for the first time, and being an American, I didn't know what to do with them. On the whole, Americans are hopeless with servants, whereas the British in the same place had no problems whatsoever; the servants were very happy. But, as an American, I didn't know how to relate as a master with servants. I couldn't even think of myself in that way. It seemed to me to be arrogant and presumptuous.

But the flaw in this idealism lies in the fact that underlying it all is a tremendous sense of insecurity and competitiveness. On one level you are being very friendly and familiar, and at the same time you are trying to prove you are better. It's a kind of hypocrisy. Without a clear hierarchy based on other values, people can be very competitive; an implicit hierarchy is set up based on material wealth. Being better is dependent on having more money—a nicer home, a better car, more of everything—because that's how you can relate in the hierarchy.

Nowadays, a relationship between a man and a woman can tend to be a competition, because there are no guidelines for mutual respect and understanding. You can see that in some marriages the husband and wife compete with each other. They feel they have to prove that one is as good as or even better than the other. But how can you have a family relationship with a competitor? The purpose of family is to live as a unit where there is harmony, where you've established enough agreement to let you relate to each other in a decent way in everyday life.

In a traditional society, the agreements are made by the society. But now, we all choose our mates—who we are going to marry, who we are going to live with, who we are going to have a relationship with. Oftentimes, we base that choice only on personal preference in the moment, rather than wise on reflection as to what kind of person would most be suitable to live with. We might choose the one who is most attractive, most charming, wealthiest, or most interesting at the moment. Or we might just need support: a man might be looking for a maternal woman, a woman who is going to replace his own mother; a woman might be looking for a father, some strong protective man who will take care of her.

Often, these desires are never really acknowledged because of our idealism. We think we are going to have the perfect relationship, based on total honesty. By "total honesty," people tend to mean saying exactly what they think whenever they feel like it, which to me is a description of a hell realm! I am really grateful that I don't say all the things I think. Sometimes what one is thinking should not be repeated; it would only cause pain, confusion, fear, and depression in the minds of those listening.

The way of mindfulness is the way of allowing ourselves to open up to the situation. Rather than waiting for the perfect person, or thinking you have to get rid of the one you are with because you're not getting on, or thinking you can find someone better, you can contemplate how to use the situation. You can reflect that this is the way it is, rather than expecting somebody to change or blaming yourself because you can't live up to your high ideals. So you become more aware of the way life actually is, the way it has to be, whether you like it or don't like it. This is the way of reflection, of mindfulness. You are not demanding happiness, or even fulfillment, from the world, but you are willing to take on the challenge that exists by beginning to work with life. Now you can only do this kind of reflection by yourself—you cannot expect someone else to tell you what you should do in your relationship, because there are so many things to take into account. Only you know them all.

For example, many people ask themselves, "Should I just live my life for myself, for my own development, even at the expense of the people who are close to me? Or should I give up any hope of ever developing myself, in order to further their welfare?" Those are the two extremes: the selfish extreme and the self-sacrificing extreme. Self-sacrificing sounds noble, doesn't it? It sounds like something we should be doing. And selfishness sounds like something we shouldn't be doing. We think it's not nice, it's wrong, to be selfish. But the Buddhist position is not an intimidating one, saying we should be totally self-sacrificing and unselfish; it encourages us to open up to that very selfishness, or to our desire to sacrifice ourselves.

We can contemplate this in our own lives. For example, rather than thinking of ourselves as selfish and then feeling guilty about it, or being caught up in the other extreme of endless giving, nurturing, and caring for others without taking any time for ourselves, we can recognize our inclination, whatever it is. Then, having recognized it, we can look at it without judging it and try to reach a balance.

Using Opposites for Spiritual Development

We can begin to see that family life can be regarded as a symbol for inner spiritual development because the family is a religious archetype. In Christian symbolism, we have God the father, Mary the mother, and Christ the child. In other religions, we might have the Divine Father and the Earth Mother symbolizing the marriage between the heavens and the earth. When you begin to really look at yourself, you find there is both a mother and a father inside, and these opposites can be reflected upon as part of your spiritual practice.

You find that just the fact that you have a female body or a male body doesn't mean that everything about you is totally female or totally male. What we need to open up to in spiritual development is the opposite; a man needs to open up to the female within, and a woman needs to open up to the male. This is not an easy thing to do, but we can use the external presence of the opposite gender to help in our practice. When a man sees a woman, or a woman sees a man, they can use the external characteristics as reminders. In a monastic community where there are monks and nuns, rather than getting involved in relationships, monks can see the external female, and they can begin to acknowledge the feminine qualities that they find internally. And for the nuns, it's the same; they can find the masculine qualities within.

My own experience as a monk, from the masculine side, is that men usually have a lot of drive; they are quite aggressive and have a lot of will power. So you often find monks becoming internally aggressive toward themselves. They try to exterminate anger, destroy fear, wipe out jealousy, and annihilate lust. But where does that get you? You get so stiff that your head aches. You become internally sterilized; you are just dried up like a desert. There is nothing, no emotion—just will power sitting there. You develop a lot of strength that way because it does take a lot of strength to maintain that attitude for any length of time, but it is also fragile, in the sense that it can be easily upset. It becomes very dependent on blind will, not on wisdom or love—not on anything that is malleable, flexible, and receptive.

So until a monk begins to open up to the inner female, he has no balance. For a man to learn to be a receptive, sensitive being, he has to stop using his will power and forcing issues all the time. He has to let go of things and become kind, gentle, and patient with himself—and with others. He needs to learn how to be extremely patient with the people he finds irritating.

One time, Ajahn Chah pointed this out to me, when I was going through one of those phases of will power. There was one monk in the monastery who really irritated me. I couldn't bear him. Just at the sound of his voice I would feel aversion arising in my mind. I asked Ajahn Chah what to do, and he said, "Ah, that monk is very good for you. He's your real friend. All those nice friends, those other *bhikkhus* that you get on so well with, they aren't very good for you. It's that one who's really going to help you." Because Ajahn Chah was a wise man, I considered seriously what he said. And I began to see that somehow I had to just totally accept that monk—accept the irritation—and let him be as he was. The masculine energy always tends to want to set someone right: "Let me tell you what's wrong with you." But to find the feminine quality of acceptance—to just sit there and let that monk be irritating and to bear with the inner irritation—I had to learn how to be patient. I began to understand what it meant to find that balance within, because I could see that I had been out of balance.

With the nuns, the imbalance tends to be the opposite. Oftentimes, women would rather be accepting of everything, no matter what it is. They are often willing to be told what they should do next. But to relate to the inner male, a woman needs to find that in herself which she can trust—that which is strong within her, that which is guiding—instead of waiting for some external authority figure to tell her what she should do. I see that it's difficult for many women to trust in their own strength. Often, they find a lack of confidence in themselves. It takes the willingness not to just wait and be receptive to things as they come, but to be firm in a situation. In general, women need to develop a sense of strength; they must trust in being wise rather than wait for some external wise person to direct them.

We need to be reminded of our opposite so we can use the external balance, the external male and female, as reminders of the internal male and female. One can use a marital relationship or a monastic situation wisely in this way. If you forget and become lost in your habitual tendencies, then whenever you see the opposite, that is a chance to remember. Rather than just seeing the opposite sex through the eyes of sexual attraction, or desire, or judgment, or just through the discriminative faculty, you can use the situation to remind yourself to open up within. That way, for a man, all women can be symbols for the internal female, so there can be a sense of respect for all women, because they represent that symbol. I assume men can serve the same symbolic function for women.

Opening to the Context of Our Life

With an attitude of openness, we are working with life as it happens. We can use the way life actually is for us—as husband or wife, teacher or pupil, parent or child—whatever our role. We need to reflect on our own situation in order to know how best to relate to our parents. Then we have to be mindful as we help our children to relate to us in skillful ways. Children need guidelines. They need to have the right suggestions, the discipline, and the conditions that will guide them toward knowing how to pay respect and toward knowing their duties as a child to their parents.

Now we should not consider duty, in this sense, to be an onerous, burdensome responsibility. Rather, it's an opportunity because we find life's joy in the duties we perform in being able to give, help, and love. It is a joy to give blessings and to be worthy of receiving them.

Noting the way society is now, we don't try to revolutionize it. We know we can't really effect much change on the general level of society at this time, but we can become clearer in our minds about ourselves. We can consider what we can do as one individual human being within the context of our life right now. Whether we are living alone, living with others, married, unmarried, happy, unhappy, with children, without children—we can begin to open our minds to the situation, rather than just react to it.

Life flows and changes, so we are called upon to open our hearts to life's flux and to learn how to adapt, rather than taking fixed positions and rigid views. We have to accept our own humanity.

That takes humor, doesn't it? Without humor, life is pretty dreadful. But with humor, and just by being more generous, open, and receptive, we can appreciate the foibles, weaknesses, and human problems we all share. We are not endlessly criticizing, demanding, and judging, neither are we just blindly wallowing in our humanity. But we are reflecting on our human condition, because we have the opportunity to transcend it. Being a monk or a nun, a parent or a child, a husband or a wife—being a human being—is not an end in itself. It's only a transition. It can never be a perfect state in itself. It's merely a convention.

Question: How about non-attachment within a relationship?

Answer: First, you must recognize what attachment is, and then you let go. That's when you realize non-attachment. However, if you're coming from the view that you shouldn't be attached, then that's still not it. The point is not to take a position against attachment, as if there were a commandment against it; the point is to observe. We ask the questions, "What is attachment? Does being attached to things bring happiness or suffering?" Then we begin to have insight. We begin to see what attachment is, and then we can let go.

If you're coming from a high-minded position in which you think you shouldn't be attached to anything, then you come up with ideas like, "Well, I can't be a Buddhist because I love my wife, because I'm attached to my wife. I love her, and I just can't let her go. I can't send her away." Those kinds of thoughts come from the view that you shouldn't be attached.

The recognition of attachment doesn't mean that you get rid of your wife. It means you free yourself from wrong views about yourself and your wife. Then you find that there's love there, but it's not attached. It's not distorting, clinging, and grasping. The empty mind is quite capable of caring about others and loving in the pure sense of love. But any attachment will always distort that.

If you love someone and then start grasping, things get complicated; then, what you love causes you pain. For example, you love your children, but if you become attached to them, then you don't really love them anymore because you're not with them as they are. You have all kinds of ideas about what they should be and what you want them to be. You want them to obey you, and you want them to be good, and you want them to pass their exams. With this attitude, you're not really loving them, because if they don't fulfill your wishes, you feel angry and frustrated and averse to them. So attachment to children prevents us from loving them. But as we let go of attachment, we find that our natural way of relating is to love. We find that we are able to allow our children to be as they are, rather than having fixed ideas of what we want them to be.

When I talk to parents, they say how much suffering there is in having children, because there's a lot of wanting. When we're wanting them to be a certain way and not wanting them to be another way, we create this anguish and suffering in our minds. But the more we let go of that, the more we discover an amazing ability to be sensitive to, and aware of, children as they are. Then, of course, that openness allows them to respond rather than just react to our attachment. You know, a lot of children are just reacting to our saying, "I want you to be like this."

The empty mind—the pure mind—is not a blank where you're not feeling or caring about anything. It's an effulgence of the mind. It's a brightness that is truly sensitive and accepting. It's an ability to accept life as it is. When we accept life as it is, we can respond appropriately to the way we're experiencing it, rather than just reacting out of fear and aversion.

17

Education for Life

The word "educate" comes ultimately from the Latin word "educere," which means "to lead forth." Knowing its etymology, we can reflect on the meaning of the word "education." If it is "something that leads forth," what is it leading us toward? When we are educating people, what is our intention? Furthermore, leading implies a kind of gentleness, doesn't it? When you lead someone, you are not forcing them. And, if you are going to lead, you have to be worthy of respect and of being followed.

Leading by Example

No one wants to learn even the finest ideals from someone who is not actually living those ideals. It would be hypocrisy. We feel averse and rebellious when someone tells us to be good and they themselves are not being good. So, if those who are educating are not worthy, then instead of leading students forth, they have to drive them. Then we have education that is geared toward compelling, bribing, and appealing to competitive instincts.

Most of us have an inclination to prove ourselves superior to others. When this is used in education, it creates a strong sense of envy, feelings of inferiority, or an attitude of superiority and arrogance. All of these are conditions of mind that lead to suffering and depression. In a competitive system, winning is the important thing, and there can be only one winner. But in a cooperative system, the aim is to lead everyone to develop their own potential so they can use their lives for the benefit of themselves and society. Therefore "leading forth" also implies that each individual should be taken into account.

In my experience with school, I observed many teachers who were not really leading. One has to make a living, so teachers are sometimes in education only for the salary. When I think of my own school days, I remember there were always a few outstanding teachers who really gave to their students and were themselves worthy of respect. But sometimes the standards in the school are not those that encourage the teachers to be worthy of leading forth. It's merely a matter of paying teachers salaries for doing their jobs during certain hours and then granting them time off. In this situation, a teacher can begin to look at education as a job—something one does to make money—rather than as something one is offering to society.

There is a need for both the teachers and the schools to see education as more than a career. Teachers don't have to be like monks or nuns, but their purpose should be one of generosity. Their intention should be to make themselves worthy of leading; they should try to be the kind of people who arouse respect and trust. This is an important reflection for our society, isn't it? Society needs to have exemplary citizens including not just monks and nuns, but also teachers, professional people, and state officials—from the prime minister or the president on down to all adults.

Beyond Vocational Training

Ideally, education should be seen as something that prepares people for life, but it is often considered to be merely a conditioning process that prepares students to read and write. It teaches them to pass examinations, get jobs, and make money while they are young. But it offers them nothing outside of that for when they get old, or for the times when they can't find jobs. Somehow education seems irrelevant to the needs of many people because it has not prepared them for anything other than getting a job.

But having a job is only part of one's life. We work only so many hours a day, and so many years of our life. And now we find that society is developing in a way that might allow us to work fewer hours or fewer years; there is a possibility now for early retirement. But this frightens many people. They say, "What will I do with my time if they retire me at fifty-five?" Buddhist monks can't retire at fifty-five. I asked the Sangha if I could retire at fifty-five, and they said, "No." But for people who are not Buddhist monks or nuns, there is the potential not to be obliged to spend an entire life working in a job. It's possible.

However, unemployment is generally regarded as a blight on society. We say, "Isn't it horrible that so many people are unemployed?" We don't say, "Isn't it wonderful that many people don't have to work in factories and in boring offices, doing routine, numbing kinds of jobs?" We don't think how wonderful that is; we think how terrible. We think we are not being fair to our youth when there is unemployment because they don't have boring, routine, unfulfilling work to do, and they are not making money. Our education makes us believe that if we aren't making money, we aren't doing anything. We are somehow inferior or worthless.

Modern education doesn't prepare us to investigate the limitations of being a human being, or to ask questions like, "What is life about? What is it for? What does it mean to be a human being living on a planet?" Such questioning requires the reflective type of thinking; we must open the mind to what we are actually feeling, thinking, experiencing, and sensing—to the limitations of our own humanity. If you don't know your limitations, then you tend to over-extend yourself and drive yourself. Or you can limit yourself with feelings of inferiority. Either extreme can lead to emotional problems.

In the human mind, we have many kinds of impulses, some worthy of respect, some not. There is the whole continuum, from the most noble impulses, to the meanest. So in our meditation and in the practice of Dhamma, we become acquainted with that in ourselves which we can respect. It is very important to find that in yourself, and to live in a way that you find worthy of respect. It's important to contemplate, "How should I live as a human being in this society? What should I do, as a mother or father, husband or wife, teacher, lawyer, businessman, merchant, craftsman, or whatever? How can I use my abilities, the qualities that I have, for a purpose that I can respect?" When there is this attitude, we are educating ourselves to learn about life and incline toward worthy pursuits; our perceptions are in harmony with what is true and good.

On the other hand, we can condition an individual human being, or a whole nation of people, to believe in the wrong things. We can be filled with superstitions, or with beliefs and perceptions of the world that are totally misguided.

This is much more possible with modern humanity than with primitive humanity. In our modern world we live in quite an artificial environment, and there is the danger that we can lose our connection to the natural processes of planetary life; we can end up living in ivory towers of delusion. We might have contempt for tribal people, feeling that they are living in a world of superstition, but we should realize that, in fact, they are very much in contact with their environment. They might perceive it in a way that is different from ours, but they are very aware of the environment they are living in and they often live in complete harmony with it.

As modern civilization develops and people are conditioned by ideas, we tend to become the slaves of the mass media. We can watch television and fill our minds with utter trivia. We can live in a world of complete artifice and totally forget the natural flow and movement of planetary life. We can even lose contact with our own bodies. If there is no antidote from our family, religious tradition, or educational system, we can lose our sense of the sacredness of life; we can become bound to gross sensual attraction, intellectual distraction, or emotional indulgence. And of course, through that, we tend to become increasingly neurotic and depressed. All the problems of modern society can be traced to our own delusions and our blind acceptance of the artifices that our society provides for us.

Now, the Buddha would always tell newly ordained monks to go off and live in the forest. What was the purpose of that? Well, what does that do to the mind when you go out and look at a forest? From my own experience, looking at nature that has been left uncorrupted, untouched by humanity's desires and fears, tends to calm me down. If you live in a forest for very long, you begin to feel calm. The things that grow there are not the kind of conditions that are deluding. They are just what they are; they are not pretending to be otherwise. Whereas so much of what humanity creates, builds, or recreates, is false, and seldom brings a sense of calm.

Teaching Our Common Humanity

Modern society has advantages, though. Because of the technology that modern civilization has produced, we now can perceive the world in universal ways. London is not very far away from Bangkok, Washington D.C., or any other place on the planet. At one time, Britain was for the British; most people were Christians, and the majority belonged to the Church of England. It was easy in those days to have a sense of national unity, with everybody sharing the same cultural attitudes, religious beliefs, and moral values. But Britain doesn't have that sense of security anymore. One no longer knows what the majority of people want, or what they feel or cherish. Nobody agrees on religion. Britain is multi-religious, multi-racial, multi-everything. And, to a certain extent, such changes are happening in every country.

This trend has advantages and disadvantages. A disadvantage is confusion. British society has ideals; it wants to do the right thing. It's certainly not a mean, selfish, or uncaring society. But it's very confused, because there is no common ground anymore. There is endless bickering and quarreling among classes and religious groups. Nobody knows how to agree on anything.

There is no common factor except our humanity. We are all human beings experiencing the same kind of suffering. We all get old, get sick, and die. We all experience anguish and despair, grief and sorrow, even though we might speak different languages, look different, eat in different ways, and react to things in different ways. So we need to bring the common ground of humanity into our consciousness, the common human experience of suffering. And this is something that needs to be emphasized in education. We need to bring this up into our own minds, and into the minds of others. We need to acknowledge this common human experience, whether it's in Ethiopia or in Buckingham Palace, in the White House or in Baghdad, the suffering is exactly the same. Men and women of all races and all nationalities have the same experiences of birth, pain, sickness, aging, and death. As humans, we are limited to a state of continuous discomfort, so most of our lives are spent just struggling to be comfortable. We try so desperately to be happy and comfortable—it becomes the whole purpose of life. But even when we feel safe and happy, we still have the same anxieties and fears. So suffering is common to all human beings.

And so is loving-kindness and compassion. The Buddhist concept of *mettā*, or loving-kindness, is the ability to be patient and bear with the imperfections in our life, our society, and ourselves. The attitude of loving-kindness is a universal value. You can have *mettā* for Christians, for Buddhists, for Jews, for every political group, and for all classes of society.

This attitude of *mettā* is not missing in any of us. It's just that we tend to overlook it when we are caught up in our frantic drives and compulsions. We are so involved in our conditioning that we miss the leveling quality of patience, forgiveness, kindness, and gentleness. But when we open ourselves, and free ourselves from the delusions of our conditioning, we come into contact with *mettā*. This is universal, whether we are educated, uneducated, male or female. This is not the prerogative of any elite class or of any religious group. The mind that is spacious and all-embracing is the common ground; it's where we see things in perspective, rather than from some extreme position.

Right education is that which leads children, adults, monks, nuns, Christians, Hindus, Muslims—the whole lot—toward what we have in common, rather than emphasizing what separates us.

Question: Why do you want to teach people about Buddhism?

Answer: Because people want to know. As a Buddhist monk, you see, I can't teach unless I'm asked. This is one of the rules of the monastic discipline. I couldn't just go up to you and say, "You should become a

Buddhist." But if you come and say, "Would you tell me about Buddhism?" or "What are you anyway? What do you believe in?" then I can tell you.

When I came to England, it was on an invitation; I was invited here by English Buddhists. I would never have come here had I not been invited. This way a monk or nun is not a missionary; we're not trying to convert anyone. But we're always making ourselves available for those who come and ask or are interested.

The tradition requires a Buddhist monk or nun to live in a way that arouses the faith of the lay community and inspires them. That means we have to live in a moral way that good people will respect. Then people are motivated to come and ask us, "What do you believe in?" or "Why do you shave your head?" And we can tell them. So it's always a process of answering questions, rather than trying to convert people or convince them of anything.

Here in the West, where there is no long tradition of Buddhism, people ask, "What good are Buddhist monks?" People can have the idea that we're just parasites on the society, that we're just loafers who don't work. They ask, "What are you doing for the peace of the world?" This kind of question comes up quite often, because the Western mind tends to see goodness as something active. But the monastic tradition is not assertive. The quality of our life occasions people to examine their own. Our presence provides the opportunity for people to question and reflect.

18
A Perfect Society

When the sun shines and everything is just as it should be, it helps us to see our mental tendency to complain or criticize. We can see that the sensory world, at its best, can only be this good. When you contemplate it, you see there is a limit to how good things can be for a human being; to know our limitations is what we call human wisdom. We need to see and contemplate these limits in order to know what is really the best we can expect on the sensory plane. Otherwise, we tend to complain, even when everything is at its best. Our ability to think and imagine gives us the potential for visualizing something even better.

Now in the same way, society can never be perfect. We can have an image or ideal for a perfect society that we can use as a guideline or goal. But we can't expect society to be perfect continuously, because part of the perfection lies in the fact that everything changes; nothing can remain the same. Just as a rose reaches its perfect fullness, perfect form, perfect fragrance and then changes, so societies reach peaks and then degenerate. This is the natural movement of all conditioned phenomena. Any sensory condition follows that pattern.

Contemplating the arising and ceasing of conditions allows us to understand them. We are not just caught in the arising and ceasing of the world—or of the human body—like a helpless creature that has no way of knowing what is beyond conditions. We actually have the ability to transcend the world, society, the body, and the self. All that we can possibly conceive of or believe in—what is most dear and precious, what is most frightening—we can transcend.

Transcendence in the Perfect Society

What do I mean by transcendence? To "transcend the world" sounds like you are somehow getting out of the whole thing by going somewhere else. To many people it would mean that you had left the world behind, that you were no longer interested in or concerned about it in any way, that you lived on a totally different plane.

But before we consider that, let's contemplate what we mean by the world. With our materialist mind, which has been conditioned through education and geography courses, we tend to see the world as a map or globe. We think the world is the planet Earth, and so to transcend the planet Earth we have to get off it somehow—perhaps we have to go up to the moon. However, when Buddhists talk about the world, we are talking about the mind, because that's what we live in. Even the concept of the planet is a concept of the mind. Any opinions we have about the world, about ourselves, about other beings, about other planets, are in fact conditions that arise and cease in the mind. Normally, we think the world is something we must seek as an external object; we say, "We'll go and study the world," meaning, we'll go to other countries on the planet. But that's not it. You don't have to go anywhere to see through the world so that you can transcend it. If you simply open your mind, you begin to notice the way things actually are, and you see that all that arises ceases.

Here on this planet, we can perceive perfection in form and color. Try to imagine forms and colors more perfect than those we see in flowers. Our precedent for perfection is what we have already perceived in form and color: we judge by what we've already seen. And yet beauty changes; it's not static. The seasons change. All the leaves fall off the trees, all the flowers disappear. Everything becomes bleak, almost monotone, in winter when there is hardly any noticeable contrast, except in the shades of dark and light. Now we might say that spring is more beautiful than winter, if we prefer vibrant colors, beautiful flowers, and the kind of energy that spring brings. But if we open our minds, we also begin to recognize the subtle beauty of winter. We can appreciate the lack of color and silence of winter as much as the energy of spring.

This appreciation comes from not having opinions about things being perfect in a static way. It comes from seeing that the rose is a perfect rose in spring, summer, autumn, and winter. For static perfection, you need a plastic rose, but that's never as satisfying. By reflecting in this way, we begin to open to the perfection of nature and the sensory world. Our view of perfection is no longer a fixed idea. We don't feel that things have to be only one way to be perfect, and we don't feel that it's the end of perfection when things change in a way that we don't like. We're not clinging to a static idea of how the world should be; instead, we see it for what it is.

Transcendence means not clinging to the world; it doesn't mean floating up into the sky away from the world. It means living within all the sensory conditions of the human form, but no longer being deluded by them. When one uses the ability to reflect and contemplate existence until one sees it clearly as it is, that is what we call transcending the world. So in transcending the world, one can still act and live in the world, but in a very clear and pure way because the world is no longer a delusion. One is not expecting the world to be anything other than what it is—and the world is the mind itself.

"*Arahant*" is the Pali term for one who has no more delusions at all about the nature of the world. That is the term we use for a perfected human being—one who has transcended the world, but who still lives in the world, working in the world for the welfare of other beings. If you have seen through the sense of self and let go of selfish interest in the world, then what else is there to do? Certainly you don't live your life for a false sense of self anymore, if that has been transcended. Someone who has total self-disinterest no longer thinks in terms of getting rewards for what they do, not even gratitude or praise. An *arahant* lives the life of a human being for the welfare of others and the society. So we could say that the perfect society would be a society of enlightened ones, *arahants* who have transcended the world.

Duties of a Wise Ruler

In reflecting on the perfect society, I think it's relevant to consider what the perfect leader, or ruler, might be like. The Pali Canon lists the ten *rājadhammā*, the virtues and duties of a wise ruler.

The first virtue is *dāna*, which means generosity or giving. Any kind of ruler—a universal monarch, a prime minister, a president, a chairman—needs to have a sense of generosity, because this is what opens the heart of a human being. Just reflect on the act of giving without expecting anything in return. When we give something we like or want to somebody else, that action opens the heart. And it always engenders a sense of nobility. Humanity is at its best when it gives what it loves, what it wants, to others.

The next virtue is *sīla*, or high moral conduct. A ruler should be impeccable in morality, a human being you can fully trust. Whether you agree with a ruler's actions or political positions isn't terribly important; it's the moral integrity of the ruler that's most important, because you can't trust someone who isn't moral. People can easily feel suspicious about someone who is not fully committed to refraining from cruelty, from killing, from taking things that have not been given, from sexual misconduct, from false speech, and from addictive drugs and drink. These standards of restraint are the basic moral precepts, the *sīla*, that you are expected to keep if you consider yourself a Buddhist.

The third virtue is *pariccāga*, or self-sacrifice. This means giving up personal happiness, safety, and comfort for the welfare of the nation. Self-sacrifice is something we need to consider. Are we willing to sacrifice personal comfort, privilege, and convenience for the welfare of our families? In the past fifty years or so, self-sacrifice has almost come to be regarded with contempt; it is put down as being foolish or naive. It seems that the tendency is to think of ourselves first, asking, "What has this government done for me? What can I get out of it?" But whenever I've thought in those ways, I've felt that I could not respect myself. In contrast, the times when I sacrificed myself, I've always felt that it was the right thing to do. Giving up personal interest, convenience, and comfort for the welfare of others—that is always something that I look back on now without regret.

The fourth virtue is *ajjava*, which is honesty and integrity. This means more than not telling lies to others; it means being honest with yourself, as well. You have to be undeluded by the desires and fears in your own mind in order to have a sense of personal honesty in which you are not blaming or condemning yourself or others or looking at the world in the wrong way.

The fifth virtue is *maddava*, which means kindness or gentleness. Living in the West, I've noticed that there is a tremendous desire for kindness and gentleness, and an idealism that reflects that desire. But what one finds in actual daily life is a kind of harshness toward oneself or others, a tendency to make harsh judgments, to react with anger, and to regard kindness as a bit soppy and wet. Gentleness is considered weak. So, in our monasteries, we've emphasized the practice of *mettā*, which is loving-kindness toward oneself and others. When we hold to high standards and ideals, we often lack kindness; we are always looking at how things should be, and we become frustrated with life as it is. This frustration can make us angry and cruel. To be kind and gentle can seem wishy-washy and weak, and yet it is a virtue that a wise ruler should have.

The sixth virtue is *tapa*, which means austerity or self-control—giving up what you don't really need. The seventh virtue is *akkodha*, which is non-anger, non-impulsiveness, calmness. This one is quite difficult because it's hard to remain calm in the midst of confusion and chaos, when things are frustrating. It's easier to act just on impulse, speaking or acting in anger.

The eighth virtue is *avihiṁsā*, which means not using violent means against anyone, not being oppressive or forcing your will on other people. Even high-mindedness can be oppressive, can't it? If you live with people who have very high standards and high ideals, they can push you down all the time with their ideas. It's a kind of violence, even though they might believe in non-violence and think they are not acting with violence. That's why we often tend to see high moral ideals as hypocrisy. When we talk about morality now, some people get very tense because they think of morality as being oppressive, as it was in Victorian times when people were intimidated and frightened by moral judgments. But that is not *avihiṁsā*. *Avihiṁsā* is non-oppression.

Next is *khanti*, which is patience, forbearance, and tolerance. To be non-oppressive and non-violent, not to follow anger, one needs to be patient. We need to bear with what is irritating, frustrating, unwanted, unloved, and unbeautiful. We need to forbear, rather than reacting violently to it, oppressing it, or annihilating it.

The last virtue is *avirodhana*, which means non-deviation from righteousness, or conformity to the law—the Dhamma. Non-deviation from righteousness sounds oppressive, doesn't it? When we become righteous, we can often become oppressive; I've seen it in myself. When I get full of righteous indignation I come at people like a demon, like the Old Testament God: "Thou shalt not!" I can be pretty frightening when I'm righteous. But *avirodhana* isn't that kind of patriarchal, oppressive righteousness; rather, it is knowing what is right, what is appropriate to time and place. In the West, we tend to believe that thinking rationally and being reasonable is right. So everything that seems rational or reasonable, we think of as right, whereas everything that is irrational or unreasonable, we see as wrong. We don't trust it. But when we attach to reason, we often lack patience, because we are not open to the movement and flow of emotion. We overlook the spaciousness of life. We are so attached to time, efficiency, quickness of thought, and the perfection of rational thinking that we view temporal conditions as reality, and we no longer notice space. So the emotional nature—the feeling, the intuitive, the psychic—all are dismissed, neglected, and annihilated.

Avirodhana, or conformity to the Dhamma, entails a steadiness in one's life that enables one to conform to the way things are. The only reason we don't conform to it is that we don't know it. Human beings are quite capable of believing in anything at all, so we tend to go every which way and follow any old thing. But once we discover the Dhamma, our only inclination is to conform to the law of the way things are.

The Wise Ruler Within

So these are the ten *rājadhammā*, the virtues of a universal ruler. We might think, "Well, that's what the prime minister or president should be doing. Maybe we should send them the list and leave it up to them."

But we can also ask, "Where within ourselves might we find the wise ruler?" This is the way of reflection.

You can apply these virtues to the practical experience of being a human being, rather than just looking at them as a way of judging the present rulers of the world. We could get into a lot of interesting criticisms, if we decided to see how much *dāna*, *sīla*, or *pariccāga* the president or prime minister has. But that would be of no value. We could figure out what *they* should do, but we wouldn't have the vaguest idea of what *we* should do—how our lives should change. Yet the more we move toward developing the wise ruler within, the more chance there is of actually getting a wise ruler outside, sometime.

We can, in daily life, move toward these virtues. They are not to be used as judgments against ourselves, to say: "Oh, I'm not generous enough; my morality isn't good enough; I'm too selfish to think of sacrificing myself." But we look at this list in order to aspire and move upward in daily life experiences. To be able to do this, we need to begin to know ourselves as we are, rather than making judgments about ourselves as we think we should be. Then, by understanding ourselves, we will understand everyone else, and we'll begin to understand society.

So, a perfect society can only happen when there are perfect human beings. And what is a perfect individual human being? One who is not deluded by the appearance of the sensory realm, one who has transcended that. When there is not a concept or an attachment to a selfish position, a selfish view, generosity becomes a natural way of relating. One wants to share. One recognizes just what is needed, and one is willing to share the extra. The tendency toward hoarding things up for oneself diminishes.

In the world today, we see a terrible discrepancy between the affluent Western world and the poverty-stricken Third World. We live at a very high standard of living, while most of the people in the world live at a very low standard. Many are not even able to get enough to eat. We can contemplate this as not being right. We can condemn the Western world, or we can try to justify our affluence and feel sorry for the Third World.

But what can we actually do about it? As individuals, we don't have enough influence with the governments and leaders of the affluent West to really change much on that level. But we can change the way we relate to the world, can't we? We can learn to practice meditation. And we can learn to live in a way whereby we become less and less selfish, so that we are willing to share what we have with others. Then we find the joy of sharing as the reward—but not an expected reward.

We can contemplate *sila*, asking ourselves what we are doing now to live in a way that is not harmful to other creatures. We can refrain from violent actions and speech, from exploitation, from all that causes division, confusion, anguish, and despair in the lives of other beings. We can practice—with our family, with our fellow workers, with our society— how to live in a way that is non-violent, that is moral, and in which we accept responsibility for what we say and do.

We can reflect on *pariccāga*, self-sacrifice. But by self-sacrifice, I don't mean a kind of soppy martyrdom where I'm sacrificing myself for this no-good lot. Self-sacrifice doesn't come from self-involvement, but from no longer regarding oneself as more important than anyone else. You have to know yourself before you can do that. The idea of sacrificing yourself without knowing yourself only makes you one of those sentimental martyrs. Self-sacrifice comes from mental clarity, not from sentimentality.

We can contemplate *ajjava*, honesty and integrity, as well as *maddava*, kindness and gentleness. We can be attentive to life in a way that is gentle and kind. The reason we lack kindness is not that we don't want to be kind; it's that we are too impatient to be kind. To be kind you have to be patient with life. To be gentle with life means you have to give in a lot; you can't just bend things and force things to fit your ideas for your own convenience, or for efficiency. Kindness means that you are learning—just in little things in daily life—to be more gentle and open, especially with things you don't like or don't want. It's easy to be open to the things you like. For example, it's easy to be kind to little children when they are being sweet and lovable, but to be kind to that which is annoying, irritating, or frustrating takes considerable attention, doesn't it? We have to put forth the effort not to react with aversion. It's very good for us to work with the irritations of daily life in little ways—to try to be gentle and kind in situations in which we are inclined to be harsh, judgmental, and cruel.

We can contemplate *tapa*—self-control, non-indulgence, austerity. Austerity is a frightening word for the modern age; it's daunting. But it's useful to ask yourself how much you really need, and how much is just an indulgence. This questioning is not passing judgment; it's beginning to note what is the right amount, noting what is necessary and what is indulgence. This takes attentiveness and honesty.

We can reflect on *akkodha*, non-anger and non-impulsiveness; *avihimsā*, non-violence and non-oppression; *khanti*, patience and forbearance; and *avirodhana*, non-deviation from righteousness. The more we are aware of these virtues, the more they can manifest in our lives.

Opening to Society's Changes

Trying to be virtuous from ideas alone can be a disaster; you just end up criticizing yourself. It's like comparing all the stages of the rose with the rose at its best, like comparing the rose in its perfect form to the bud and the decayed rose. This type of comparison makes us say, "I don't like this; that is how everything should be." But when we see that the sensory world is a process—that it's continually changing—we begin to appreciate it in all its forms. We no longer want to fix it in a static way, judging everything according to the fixed view that we have about it.

We can apply this perspective to our society and also to ourselves. We realize that even though society will never be perfect, it will—like the rose—reach its peak. Then we might contemplate our society and ask, "What stage has it reached? Is it at its peak? Is it past its peak?" We could say, "It's no good, it's not like it used to be, it shouldn't be like this," and go on like this endlessly, getting depressed and hating it because it's not at its peak. But it's more useful to simply ask, "Where is it?" As we open ourselves to society's as well as our own changes—to the law, to the Dhamma—we can flow with society in a way that will give it the strength to be healthy.

—ᴍ—

Question: Does Buddhism favor one type of society over another? For example, does it recommend democracy over monarchy?

Answer: In Buddhism there is no particular attempt to describe how the perfect society should operate; as a monarchy or a democracy, as a socialist or communist state. In the Buddha's time, there probably weren't many choices. Monarchy tended to be the way, though there were natural democracies, also. But even monarchy in those days was not an oppressive system in which the king had the divine right to do anything he wanted at the expense of everyone else. Nowadays, we are conditioned to think that monarchs are degenerates who are all corrupt—that a monarchy is just for the privileged few and everyone else has to pay for it and suffer—but actually, the theory of monarchy always stemmed from righteousness. It wasn't intended to be an oppressive system, though in many cases it became that, just as communism and democracy can become oppressive systems.

Western democracy, with all its so-called freedom, tends to bring us toward degeneration. Parents now worry about their children endlessly. They have lost all ability to direct their children in skillful ways because children now have the freedom to do anything they want. It seems we no longer have the right to guide or direct anyone toward what is right and good and beautiful. We just say, "You are free to do what you want." Also, communism, with all its high-minded idealism, actually tends to oppress. It seems to take all these lovely ideas of sharing, equal distribution, equality, and so on, and just shove them down your throat. That is certainly not what we mean as the goal for a Buddhist society.

But in fact, all the existing structures would be workable if we had the right understanding. There is nothing really wrong with the current political structures; government agencies are quite all right in themselves. What is missing is the enlightened human being, the human being who sees clearly.

19

A Matter of Life and Death

For those who practice the Dhamma, life is a time for contemplation and reflection on the way things are. Even the death of our loved ones is part of our contemplation. We recognize that having been born means that we're going to separate from each other, that we'll see the death of those we know, and that we'll all die, eventually. So this involvement with life and death is Dhamma for us. It's the way things are; there's nothing wrong with it.

Our society refuses to accept and really contemplate death. We are so involved with life and trying to make everything nice during our lifetime that we tend to ignore the finale of life. So we're totally unequipped for it. If you think of what the most important events in a human life are, you realize they are birth and death. Well, the idea of birth—of having babies—is dear to the hearts of people, but the idea of death is baffling. What happens when somebody dies? What does it mean?

The very perception of death leaves us in a state of not knowing exactly what's happened. What happened to that person we once perceived as being alive? Where did he go? Did he go anywhere, or is death just oblivion? Heaven, hell, oblivion—does anybody know?

What we can know is that we don't know. We can know that we're still alive, and we haven't died yet, and we can know that we don't know what happens when somebody dies. Now this may not seem like a lot, but it is very important, because what most people fail to understand is that they don't know. Instead, some people will believe anything, they'll settle for anything, any kind of speculation or creepy idea.

Dying Before Death

The way of meditation is the way to die before your body dies. It's a way of dying before death and dying to death so that, poetically speaking, death is dead, rather than anything else. By "death," I'm talking about that perception in the mind. If the perception of death is taken personally, then we become frightened because we think we're going to die. Our perception of being alive is based on the view that this body is mine and that I am this body—so the perception of death is frightening. We live in a world of anxiety and fear over the death of our bodies, separation from what we love, or the mystery of what happens when we die. We wonder, "Is it worth being good, following moral precepts, and being kind? Or should we not be bothered because it doesn't matter? Is this universe without any moral principles, so that you can murder and steal and lie and cheat because it doesn't really matter? After death, is it just oblivion, or do our actions in this human form affect what happens next?" Well, we could speculate about these questions for the rest of our lives!

However, the Buddha pointed not to any speculation about life and death but to the way things are in our living experience. And this is what meditation is about. It's an investigation, an examination, a profound looking into the way things are. We examine what the body is, what our feelings are, and what makes us feel joy and serenity. We see for ourselves what desire and attachment really are, and we watch conditions arise and cease.

Dying before death is allowing that which has arisen to cease. This teaching is about the mind; we'll let the body die when it's time for it to die. If it lives another minute, or another fifty years, or another eighty years, or whatever—that's up to the body. We're in no hurry to die, nor are we trying to live longer than necessary. We allow this body to live its lifespan, because it's not self; it does not belong to us. However long this body breathes and lives is all right. It's not mine anyway. But during the time that it's alive, there's an opportunity to die before death: to die to ignorance and selfishness; to die to greed, hatred, and delusion; to let all these things die; to let them go and let them cease.

So one is observing death as it's really happening, as the ending, the cessation of these things we tend to regard as ourself, but are merely mortal conditions.

Human beings tend to interpret every form of greed, hatred, and delusion as a personal thing. We think, "I'm greedy, I'm angry, I'm deluded. And because I am, you are." So the I-am-you-are conviction creates the illusion of my being a personality. But what is personality, what is self, what is it really? We can observe the fear of letting go of our personality when we notice the subtle thought, "If I'm not obsessed with myself, then what's going to be left? I'll dissolve and disappear into a void. If I don't make a lot of *kamma* for myself—have interesting neurotic problems, go to psychiatrists, spend hours talking about my fears and anxieties, make emotional attachments—what then?" We can see how afraid we are of letting go of our personality.

Family relationships provide a good example. If you have children, you might say, "How can I not be attached to my children?" Well, you don't have to throw your children into a crater to convince yourself you're not attached to them! Letting selfishness die doesn't mean that you don't love your children. It means you're no longer attached to the perception of you as someone whose happiness is dependent on the belief that these children are yours, that they love you, that they can't live without you, and that you can't live without them. We can create a whole sticky web of delusion about children. We call it "loving our children" when actually, that love is caught up in the web of attachment and ignorance. Very little love can really happen in that kind of relationship.

So love doesn't mean attachment. It means being able to see clearly, to be joyous and selfless, to give freely, and to serve others without selfish interests. It's being able to live without the views of me and mine, and without the kind of misery that we can create around our parents, our children, our husband, our wife, our friends—our world.

Perhaps death is the awakening from the dream of life. Have you ever thought of it like that? Life lived with a self-view can be a living death, a continuous kind of misery and fear that swarms within our minds. Depression is death; despair is death; fear, desire, and ignorance are death. So we can live a living death—or we can die to death before we die, by awakening from the dream of life and from the illusions of a self.

The Only Real Certainty

We have to accept the limitations of being born in a body. We have to bear with the seeming separateness that this gives us, and also with the sense of being pulled toward the objects of the senses all the time. This is just part of the *kamma* of birth. These bodies having been born, this is the way it is. But we're not judging it, saying it's mine, or that it should be this way or that way. Instead, we're noting. This takes mindfulness—the ability to observe and be open-minded—in order to see how it really is. So this sensory world as it is, as we experience it within the lifespan of this body, is our Dhamma practice. It's always teaching us; it's always our refuge and teacher.

As you can see, this way of reflection is a kind of turnabout from the worldly attitude. Death is generally considered a tragedy, something terrible and frightening; sometimes it's considered morbid even to think about it. Yet to me, it seems very important to reflect on it because it's something that's going to happen to me. The only real certainty in life is death. All these bodies will die. The death of this body is one of the important events in this life. In our meditation, we're learning how to die; we're learning how to allow things to flow according to their nature, how to be open, receptive, and in harmony with the way things are. And "the way things are" includes all that we experience within our lives—even the illnesses, the aging process, and death.

Even if you should be in perfect health from birth to death, that does not prevent aging and death. So we investigate old age, sickness, and death, not for any morbid reason but because these are the very processes we're involved with. It's ridiculous to think about butterflies and Persian miniatures all our life and ignore the very fundamental processes of human existence. When I'm dying, I don't imagine a butterfly is going to be much consolation or of any great import.

What's Really Important

In our monasteries, we've had the opportunity to be with several people as they were dying. What has been important for each of them was the Dhamma. It wasn't how much money they'd made, or the achievements of their worldly life, or their failures. At the time of death, all of these things seem so irrelevant, so totally unimportant. But what is important is the Dhamma: the ability to reflect, to contemplate, and to meditate on the way it is.

Everything is changing and moving in its own way: the changing nature of the body, the way it ages, the days, the nights, and the seasons of the year. Some things move quickly, and some things move slowly; but what we're beginning to notice in meditation is this changing energy. We're cultivating awareness of change in our lives, rather than just putting in time—doing things, and then deluding ourselves that our personal achievements are important and urgent. If you follow that way of living, by the time you get old and are ready to die, you won't know what really happened to your life. You will have been just putting in time, waiting for death to come.

The contemplative mind stays with the way things are, with the movement and change of energy. So it's no longer me waiting for death, or me just putting in time and getting through life somehow as best I can. There is mindfulness and there is investigation, which allow us to see things as they are. We are letting go of illusions and can begin to see the end of suffering.

If we're not aware of what life is about, we get confused. We say, "Why me? Why do I have to get old? Why do I have to have arthritis? Why do I have to be in this nursing home? It's not fair. If there really were a God, He would have made it so that I could be fit as a fiddle my whole life and die in perfect health. I'd just suddenly go to sleep and not wake up—no pain, no misery, no disgusting things happening. I'd have a perfect death, and I would never feel embarrassed or be a burden. I'd always be at my cleanest, nicest, most acceptable, and most pleasing."

But we know, don't we, what's going to happen, and a lot of it's not very pretty, very clean, or nice. But it's Dhamma, isn't it? It's the way things are. We begin to appreciate all of the Dhamma—not just the nice side of it—because we're seeing it in perspective, through the awakened mind and through wisdom, rather than through the self. The self will always be saying, "Oh, I don't want to be a burden on anybody; I don't want to have to lose control of my bowels. It'll be terribly embarrassing." That's self-view. It's misery, isn't it, because life doesn't go the way you want. And even if it does go the way you want, you still worry about it. You think, "What if?" You know it's all right now, but anything could happen. And that's a thought that causes suffering.

Life is fraught with dangers, and the self is always in danger. It's dangerous to be selfish. So actually, the death of the self is relief—*nibbāna*. It's release from danger, from struggle and strife, and from all the suffering that we produce out of the illusion of self. We live in a world, in a society, that holds to that illusion, but in Dhamma practice, we're challenging that illusion. We're not just trying to be clever and dismiss it, but are investigating: "Is this really the way it is? Is this the real truth? What is the truth?" And we're no longer looking for someone to come along and tell us the truth, because we know that we have to realize it for ourselves. The truth is here and now, to be seen by each of us for ourselves through the practice of mindfulness and wisdom.

An Occasion for Openness

When people have died in our monasteries over the past years—people with terminal illnesses—the monks and nuns nursed them through their death. Since I had never done that before, the experience was a revelation to me. I actually found it quite joyful. Ordinarily, we imagine the experience of death as so negative that we think, "Somebody's dying. I don't want to see. I don't want to go. I'd rather go anywhere else."

One woman who came to die—a Thai woman—was about forty-three years old, and she had terminal cancer. She was a meditator, and she was very open about what was happening to her. She took ordination as a nun when she was dying, and the nuns took care of her. The monks would also sit with her sometimes, and meditate with her.

Her Thai friends used to come from London to see her, and they'd ask how she was. I'd say, "She's really wonderful." And they'd say, "Oh, is she getting well?" They were surprised when I answered, "No." They couldn't see how she was very beautiful and very pure in her dying state. They just felt that if she was dying, that was terrible. But when you were actually with her, you didn't feel negative. You weren't eager for her to die; you would rather she lived, so there was a kind of sadness involved, but it wasn't depressing. Then, when she actually died, the community was very uplifted by it.

Even though cultural perceptions of death have negative connotations, it is actually not at all depressing or horrible when there is the ability to open to it. To be with someone who is dying can even be inspiring when you encourage that kind of openness within the dying person and within yourself.

Question: Is the death experience important in Theravadan Buddhism?

Answer: Yes, contemplation of death is considered to be contemplation of the way things are, of the laws of nature. What I appreciated in Thai funerals was that they became a contemplation. You weren't speculating about where the soul was. You were just reflecting on the experience of somebody dying. You'd look at the corpse, and you'd contemplate a dead body. You weren't projecting anything onto it, such as ugliness. You could just watch how you actually reacted to it. If you'd never seen a human corpse before, and if it was rotting, then you'd tend to say: "It's ugly. I can't stand the smell. This is horrible." But as you got beyond that, as you stopped just reacting negatively toward it, you'd find that even the presence of the corpse was quite calming. It's a natural process of decay, and it's quite marvelous. You find that nature, even in its decaying forms, is part of the perfection. There's nothing bad or foul, outside of your own projections.

One time I went to a hospital in Bangkok where they would let the monks contemplate corpses. This time they had a bloated corpse that they had found in one of the canals. It had been dead about a week, and it was really foul and putrid, all bloated with gases, and maggots were coming out of its eyes. The smell and the appearance were really horrendous at first. The reaction was total aversion and wanting to get out. You had to make yourself approach it; you had to use your will. And then you had to stand there accepting the corpse for what it was, even the odor and appearance.

But then something changed. Once the aversion and negativity stopped, once you got through that, you began to contemplate it as Dhamma and to appreciate it. You could appreciate that process as being perfect, realizing it as the perfection of nature. It's a natural process, and it's not bad or hideous. It's about life and the way things move and change. When you can see the decaying process from a calm clarity, then you begin to see nature as Dhamma.

In Thailand the word for nature is "Dhamma." They call it "Dhammachat." It means the natural way of things, the laws of nature. But in the West, we tend to have the idea that nature is something outside of religion. There's a metaphysical structure in Christianity that doesn't have much to do with the natural law. So salvation is dependent on believing in metaphysical doctrines, rather than on understanding the natural law. According to the way I was conditioned, nature is something out there; it's what you see. There are mountains and trees, and there are natural laws, but they have very little to do with you, so you tend to feel like an alien.

But your body operates on the natural laws; it's part of a planetary structure. And the whole process is part of a perfect whole. In Buddhism, when you equate Dhamma with the natural way of things, you're opening your mind to the way things are. That's what the Buddha discovered when he became enlightened: he realized the natural way of things. And all of the false views of self and culture that are based on ignorance, fear, and desire, simply dissolved in his mind.

20
Toward the Future

Reflecting on the future is important for us. The future is what hasn't happened yet; it's the unknown. It's the potential for what could happen, whether for good fortune or bad, for pleasure or pain. As Buddhists, we contemplate the future because we recognize that what we do in the present moment establishes the causes of what will happen to us in the future. The teaching is simple: when we do good, we receive good, and when we do bad, we receive bad. This is the law of cause and effect, or kamma. If we live now in a way that is harmful, unkind, and selfish, it brings a bad result in the future. With an understanding of *kamma,* we know that it's important now to take on the responsibility for how we live, what we do, and what we say. We know that it's important to live this life in the human form in the right way.

The Unknown Future

The future—what is your perception of that? When you think about the future, what happens to your mind? Just ask yourself: what do you want to happen? What do you fear or dread, expect or hope? These are the conditions we create about the future, aren't they? Expectation, speculation, guessing, hoping, longing, dreading, fearing, anticipating— these are the mental states we create about the future because the future is unknown. We speculate a lot about the future. Some people go to clairvoyants or fortune-tellers, and then they can say, "Maybe this will happen, or maybe that will happen."

But the mode of meditation is not speculation. We are observing how things actually are, and what we recognize is that the future is unknown. It's something vast and infinitely mysterious, with the potential for anything—from the best to the worst.

But often, because we know that our bodies will die and we will be separated from what we love, the future involves dread in the mind. We don't want to think about it too much, because it reminds us of death and separation. Our attachment to life, as we are experiencing it, makes us frightened of death. We become so attached to our life—to the human form we are in, to the people we love, to the things we have, and to the world as we perceive it—that the whole thought of being separated from it can be very anguishing to us. So we hang desperately onto life, onto other people, onto things, onto a sense of stability and safety, only to have it all inevitably snatched away from us as time goes by. So death for us is one of the most frightening mysteries.

Nowadays, people like to speculate about what happens when people die. The materialist's view is that you die and that's the end. The reincarnationist's view is that our soul is reborn in a different form. Some religious views propose a celestial heaven and a subterranean hell. But what you have to admit to yourself is that you don't know what happens, because you haven't died yet. The future is unknown, but you are very much involved with existence in a living form at this time. So what we must come to terms with now is this existence, this life, within the changing mortal conditions of sensory consciousness.

Rather than speculate about what will happen in the future when the body dies, the Buddha pointed to the fact that within this limitation of human consciousness, the way out of suffering is by being aware of the way things are now. That is the way out of birth in the mind. And the way out of birth is also the way out of death, because you cannot have death without birth. The Buddha's teaching is always pointing to the way out of being reborn in the present moment—even though the body is still existing, still breathing, still able to think and feel and sense and experience. With Right Understanding, there is no rebirth coming from ignorance; there is only the natural movement and flow of consciousness and the peace of just knowing, rather than the fear and desire that come from ignorance. And with Right Understanding, there is openness and trust with which to approach the unknown future.

Right View, the right way of seeing things, is a completely fearless way because it is infinite. It is eternal. It is something truly grand and miraculous. Because we can't perceive it, all we can do is open to it, open the mind to the unknown, the mystery. This can be terrifying. The religious experience is often described as a terrible one, which means that it is terrifying. It is taking away, pulling away, everything that you identify with and depend on, everything you feel safe and comfortable with. Suddenly, it's all removed, ripped away from you, and you are left with nothing. But the marvelous thing about it is that, when you can accept it, that is where you find true peace. It is truly peaceful to be completely open, totally vulnerable and alert, to the mystery of the unknown.

In addition to speculating about the future, we often build defenses to protect ourselves against it. But by increasing our defenses, we are just increasing the amount of fear and anxiety. Yet we think that is the way to safety. We think we've got to make ourselves so strong that no one will dare attack us, but that attitude demands endless propping up, doesn't it? And our defenses inevitably fail us. We can look mean and flex our muscles a bit, but we can't stand with muscles flexed all the time. We have to relax. And when we do, somebody can catch us in a position in which we are quite vulnerable. All the defenses we can build are no protection against the unknown.

Total Openness, Total Trust

One definition of the religious experience is making yourself totally vulnerable, with no protection at all; not even asking God to help you; not saying, "Please help me" when somebody is attacking you; being able to be totally vulnerable and totally sensitive to the planet, the universe, the grand mystery. To me, this is the whole purpose and ultimate perfection of human life. We begin to see that the only way out of suffering is not by protecting ourselves, but by allowing ourselves to be completely open.

Our society is very interested in protection against the unknown. It offers insurance, retirement benefits, and all kinds of safeties and securities that we demand and expect. And yet, the Buddhist religious life is exemplified by the monk, an alms mendicant who is totally dependent and defenseless, a little bit odd, a little bit outside of everything, who wears orange robes and has a shaven head. The conventions of a monk's life are merely external symbols representing what we need to do internally. To internalize that monk or mendicant means that you must be willing to trust in the Dhamma, in the truth. The more you practice meditation, the more you have insight into the way things actually are, and the more joy, faith, and confidence you feel. The more you practice, the more willing you are to completely open yourself to the mystery, to the vastness, to the awesomeness—without trembling.

As human beings, we are vulnerable little creatures. In contrast to the universe, we are weak and soft. For example, we have very delicate skin that's easily damaged. But in spite of our vulnerability in the midst of a vast and mysterious universe, one can feel total trust. From my own insight, through meditation, I know that there is total trust now. There is complete confidence in the benevolence and wonder of the universe.

One can't really perceive the whole, vast universe in any clear way; one can only open to it. Ordinarily, human consciousness is limited to the perceptions we have through our senses; it's very difficult for us to catch glimpses beyond that. But the more we let go of our grasping of the sensory world—the less we hold onto it and identify with it—the more we begin to have glimpses of deathlessness. We begin to experience *amaravati*, the deathless realm, the underlying unity, the overlying compassion, the whole wondrous miracle.

It's part of the human condition that, in spite of our obvious limitations as individual creatures, we have an ability to comprehend the whole. But that comprehension comes, not from the perception of the whole, but from the opening of the heart. We are not just trying to believe in a perception of wholeness that we hold as a doctrine. We are going to the very experience of wholeness, as we open the heart. This is fearlessness. It is the willingness to be hurt, to be totally sensitive, and to bear with the pain, despair, and confusion of our sensory experience.

So the future is unknown. As spiritual seekers, we turn toward the unknown. Rather than constantly hanging on to the known in our meditation, more and more we begin to open our heart to the unknown. We relish that, we long for that: just the simple openness of heart and the willingness to bear with life as we are experiencing it—with all its ups and downs, good fortune, bad fortune, pleasure, and pain. We are no longer crying for God to protect us and help us and send us good fortune. We are no longer expecting a life that offers only good health and pleasure. We'll take whatever comes, whatever it is. This is the way we approach the future, not by looking for protection, but by opening our hearts.

—∞—

Question: If calamity does strike someone, how do you suggest they deal with it?

Answer: I would suggest that they try to really accept the way it is. They can bring it into consciousness, rather than pushing it aside, indulging in emotion, or resisting it. They can try to just notice and accept that this is the way it is, and to bear the feeling of sorrow or sadness that's there. Then they'll be able to let it go. Letting it go doesn't mean that it will go away when they want it to, but it means that they won't be making any problems about it.

Life is like this. All of us, all human beings, experience the loss of someone they love. It's just part of our human condition, and human beings have always experienced that. We have to watch our parents die. Maybe we have to experience the death of a child or a good friend. Sometimes we have to accept horrendous things in life. But when we are mindful, we have already accepted all possibilities. One still feels the anguish, but one can accept that feeling. That acceptance has its own peacefulness, too; the experience of life has a sad quality to it.

Every morning in the monastic community we chant, "All that is mine, beloved and pleasing, will become otherwise." You might think this is a horrible thing to say, but it's a reflection on the fact that what we love, what pleases us, is going to change. We suffer when we think it shouldn't change, and when we don't want any changes. But if our mind is open to life, then we often find that it is in the times when we suffer that we also grow. People whose lives have been too easy sometimes never grow up; they become rather spoiled and complacent. It's when you've really had to look at and accept painful things that you find yourself growing in wisdom and maturing as a person.

I was invited to give talks to people with AIDS in the San Francisco area of California. Of course, that is a very traumatic disease and has all kinds of ugly things connected with it. Having your immune system break down is probably one of the most miserable things that can happen to a human being. So there is the tendency to take it all personally, with bitterness and resentment, or with guilt and remorse. You could interpret it as "God's justice," punishing you for living an immoral life. You could feel mistreated by life, hating God because he gave you this terrible thing. You could shake your fist at the heavens and feel self-pity and blame. Or, on the other hand, you could look at the experience as a chance for awakening to life, a chance to really look and understand.

When you know you're going to die, sometimes that can make the quality of the remainder of your life increase considerably. If you know you're going to die in six months, and you have any wisdom at all, you're not going to go around wasting those six months on frivolities. If you're perfectly healthy, you might think, "I've still got years ahead of me. No point in meditating now, because I can do that when I'm older. Right now I'm going to have a good time." In one way, knowing you're going to die in six months can be a very painful realization, but in another way, it can awaken you to life. That's the important thing—the awakening and the willingness to learn from life—no matter what you've done or what's happened. Every one of us has this ever-present possibility for awakening, no matter what we may have done.

I see our life in this human form as a kind of transition. We don't really belong here. This is not our real home. We're never going to be content with our state as human beings. It's not worth lingering or hanging around in the human realm, but it's not to be despised or rejected either. Our human life is to be awakened to and understood. You can say you've not wasted your life if you awaken to it. If you live a long life—say one hundred years—following foolish ideas and selfishness, then one hundred years have been wasted. But if you've awakened to life—even if your life is very short—then at least you've not wasted it.

About the Author

AJAHN SUMEDHO, a monk for over forty years, studied closely with the renowned meditation master Ajahn Chah (author of *Food for the Heart*) and established the first Theravadan monastic community in the West. Though he is a seminal figure in Western Buddhism, much of Sumedho's work has not been widely available. The author of *The Sound of Silence*, he lives in England.

Amaravati Buddhist Monastery

Amaravati Buddhist Monastery was founded by Ajahn Sumedo in 1984. Situated in Hertfordshire, England, Amaravati was opened in response to the need for increased facilities for women who had undertaken the training as nuns, and to provide further accomodation for bhikkhus and a venue for large numbers of lay people.

Since its inception, Amaravati, which means "the Deathless Realm," has become a monastic residence for approximately thirty ordained people. The monastery comprises a large interfaith library; facilities for retreats and meditation classes, guided by monks and nuns of the community; and accomodation for lay people to stay as guests or as long-term residents. As well as hosting seminars and conferences on a variety of themes, Amaravati also sponsors traditional Theravadan Buddhist festivals and regular events for families.

Amaravati Buddhist Monastery
Great Gaddesden
Hemel Hempstead, Herts HP1 3BZ
England
Telephone: 01442-842455
amaravati.org

Wisdom Publications

Wisdom Publications, a nonprofit publisher, is dedicated to making available authentic works relating to Buddhism for the benefit of all. We publish books by ancient and modern masters in all traditions of Buddhism, translations of important texts, and original scholarship. Additionally, we offer books that explore East-West themes unfolding as traditional Buddhism encounters our modern culture in all its aspects. Our titles are published with the appreciation of Buddhism as a living philosophy, and with the special commitment to preserve and transmit important works from Buddhism's many traditions.

To learn more about Wisdom, or to browse books online, visit our website at www.wisdompubs.org.

You may request a copy of our catalog online or by writing to this address:

Wisdom Publications
199 Elm Street
Somerville, Massachusetts 02144 USA
Telephone: 617-776-7416
Fax: 617-776-7841
Email: info@wisdompubs.org
www.wisdompubs.org

The Wisdom Trust

As a nonprofit publisher, Wisdom is dedicated to the publication of Dharma books for the benefit of all sentient beings and dependent upon the kindness and generosity of sponsors in order to do so. If you would like to make a donation to Wisdom, you may do so through our website or our Somerville office. If you would like to help sponsor the publication of a book, please write or email us at the address above.

Thank you.

Wisdom is a nonprofit, charitable 501(c)(3) organization affiliated with the Foundation for the Preservation of the Mahayana Tradition (FPMT).

Wisdom Publications

199 Elm Street
Somerville, MA 02144 USA

Please return this card if you would like to be kept informed about our current and future publications.

Name

Street

City_____State_____Zip (Postal Code)

Country_____Email

In which book did you find this card?

How did you find out about this book?

□ Website
□ Magazine   □ Library   □ Other

visit us at
www.wisdompubs.org for discounts and special offers

Wisdom Publications is a nonprofit charitable organization.